Celtic Angels

Celtic Angels

True Stories of Angel Blessings
from Ireland to the World

Theresa Cheung

**SIMON &
SCHUSTER**

London · New York · Sydney · Toronto · New Delhi

A CBS COMPANY

First published in Great Britain by Simon & Schuster UK Ltd, 2012
A CBS COMPANY

1 3 5 7 9 10 8 6 4 2

Simon & Schuster UK Ltd
1st Floor
222 Gray's Inn Road
London WC1X 8HB

www.simonandschuster.co.uk

Simon & Schuster Australia, Sydney
Simon & Schuster India, New Delhi

A CIP catalogue record for this book is available
from the British Library.

ISBN: 978-1-84983-483-4

Typeset by Hewer Text UK Ltd, Edinburgh
Printed and bound by CPI Group (UK) Ltd, Croydon, CR0 4YY

Contents

Acknowledgements   vii

Irish Angel Blessing   ix

Introduction: Angels Knocking at My Heart   xi

Chapter One: The Stranger Who Changed My Life   1

Chapter Two: Anam Cara   23

Chapter Three: Divine Visitors   61

Chapter Four: Celtic Souls   102

Chapter Five: The Land of the Young   150

Chapter Six: Celtic Hearts   201

Chapter Seven: Angel Inspirations   250

Acknowledgements

Like all the angel books I have had the privilege to write over the years, this book was a labour of love from start to finish and just would not have been possible without the help of some wonderful people. I espccially want to thank my agent, Clare Hulton, for her advice and encouragement, my editor Kerri Sharp for her insight and vision, and everyone at Simon and Schuster for being so very helpful throughout the entire process of writing this book and getting it ready for publication.

Once again, I would like to take this opportunity to thank from the bottom of my heart everyone who has written to me over the years to share their inspiring angel stories and insights. I'm deeply indebted to you all because you truly are the soul, heart and spirit of every angel book I write, and it gives me great joy to know that your words and thoughts will bring comfort and hope to all those who read my books.

Special thanks again go to Ray, Robert and Ruthie for their love and support and for being the earth angels that you are. Thanks also to Blanca for her research contribution and for her support and encouragement. And last, but certainly not least, sincere thanks to everyone who reads this book. I hope it will help you rediscover the Celtic soul within you and open your heart to the angels that are always around you, and forever within you.

Irish Angel Blessing
May you always walk in sunshine.
May you never want for more.
May Irish angels rest their wings right beside your door.

Introduction: Angels Knocking at My Heart

*It is often when we are not searching
That we find the most valuable treasures.*

Anon

If you know me, or have read one of my other angel books, *An Angel Called My Name, An Angel Healed Me, An Angel Changed My Life, An Angel Spoke to Me, An Angel Saved Me* or *How to See Your Angels,* you will know that I believe angels to be real. I believe that this life does not end in death and that each and every one of us has a guardian angel that watches over us in this life and the next.

I've spent the best part of twenty-five years researching the paranormal and I am also absolutely convinced that our guardian angels can express themselves to us in countless different ways. On very rare occasions they may manifest their loving presence in their traditional wings-and-halo-guise, but since the definition and true power of faith is to believe without tangible proof they are far more likely to reveal themselves in subtle, gentle, invisible but deeply personal ways. Beings of light can, for instance, materialise in our dreams or in coincidences or unexpected sparks of intuition that seem to come out of nowhere. They may choose to express themselves through the unconditional love of beloved pets. The natural world is another common place for angels to leave their calling cards, perhaps in rainbows, feathers, clouds, sunsets or birdsong. They may also make themselves known to us through a hug, a smile, a song, or anything that heals or lifts our spirits.

Yet another common way for heaven to reassure us of the angels' constant presence is through sudden and unexpected feelings of connection with the spirits of departed loved ones. And last, but by no means least, they may reveal themselves through the words or actions of other people, consciously or unconsciously guided from above. And never discount the truth that sometimes it may be our own selfless words and deeds that play a part in bringing heaven closer to earth. Indeed, anyone who is blessed with the ability to live their life with a sense of the divine presence in everyone and everything could well be the vital ingredient angels need to manifest their loving presence on earth. In other words, angels need us to help them, just as much as we need them.

In my previous angel books I had the privilege and honour to collect together true-life stories from people who believe they have seen angels. Although the stories came from all corners of the world, I soon began to notice that a fairly substantial proportion featured the experiences of Irish people, or were related to Ireland in some way. I could see a definite trend emerging, but a far more prominent theme I noticed was that regardless of any connection with the Emerald Isle, people who encountered angels in their daily lives, or believed angels were watching over them, had (whether they consciously realised it or not) what I like to call a Celtic soul. And by that I mean they had an awareness of magic that penetrated every aspect of their lives, both ordinary and extraordinary. I also began to see how this magical approach to life was strikingly similar to the spirituality of the ancient Celts.

I've been writing about the paranormal for over two decades now and looking back I can see that almost from the very beginning this Celtic soul theme was emerging. The more I researched and gathered information and stories for my psychic world encyclopaedias and angel books the more I discovered parallels between ancient Celtic spirituality and the angel movement as it is revealing itself to us today. It also became clear, as more and more stories from Ireland were sent to me, that I had a great deal to learn from the innate ability of many Irish people to 'see' the world spiritually. Scepticism, doubt and fear simply weren't as prominent in their world-view. Perhaps all along these people and their awesome stories and insights were the angels knocking at my heart.

God-intoxicated

The Irish have always seemed to be an extraordinary race – 'God-intoxicated' is how they are often described. For them there is no division between this life and the next. Heaven is constantly shining through everyday reality and everyone and everything carries a blessing. It is this sense of the immanent presence of spirit and the discovery of the extraordinary in the ordinary that gives the Irish a perception of magic that infuses all aspects of their lives.

Without doubt, this sense of divine potential in the everyday is a characteristic of many Irish people but it is by no means restricted to the Irish. Regardless of race or culture there is a part deep within us all that searches for meaning and magic in life. It is the part of us that is intuitive, creative, passionate, spontaneous and imaginative, but it is also the part of us most in need of comfort, guidance, love and reassurance and the part of us most likely to be forgotten and neglected as we grow older and more cynical and burdened down with responsibilities. In this book, I will be referring to the deep-rooted magical but vulnerable part within each one of us as our Celtic soul, or *anam cara*, meaning 'soul friend' in Gaelic, but you may want to call it your angel within, your inner child, your sixth sense or your intuition, or indeed any name that speaks to your spirit. Whatever you decide to call it, in our increasingly secular world many of us lose touch with the magic within us, but I want to reassure you that it remains with us all our lives. Each and every one of us at some time in our lives longs to find a sense of higher purpose and meaning and it is through this longing that our guardian angels will constantly try to connect with us. All we need to do is open our hearts and listen.

According to the Swedish mystic Emanuel Swedenborg, there is no need to look outside of ourselves to encounter angels, because at every moment angels are within us, waiting to open our eyes and our hearts to the world of spirit. Our inner angel should therefore be looked on as our best friend, adviser and guide throughout our journey in this life and the next; our *anam cara*, our soul friend.

This book aims to show that it is through our inner guardian angel that heaven first reaches out to us. In this way, with love, trust and an open soul, anyone can see, hear or sense the nearness of their guardian angel. Therefore in the pages that follow not only will you find remarkable stories from or about Irish people, but you will also find miraculous stories from or about people who don't have any connections with Ireland as such. The thread linking all the stories together is that the people who submitted them all have the ability to 'see' the world spiritually, and whether they are Irish or not, whether they realise it or not, they have Celtic souls. Seeing the world with angel eyes does not mean seeing the world through rose-coloured spectacles, or being impressionable or gullible, it means having an open mind and heart, the ability to feel things deeply and the courage to suspend disbelief, and it is this openness and spontaneity that attracts beings of pure spiritual light to us.

Real-life stories

Another thread linking all these stories together is that they are real-life stories, based in fact and not fantasy. The first chapter discusses some of my own experiences. You'll see that even though I was born into a family of psychics and spiritualists, and am now a firm believer in an afterlife, I still had so very much to learn about life in spirit when I made my first trip to Ireland five years ago. You'll also see that I have had many moments of intense doubt and uncertainty and it has taken me many decades, indeed a lifetime, to trust in my angels.

I feel it is important for you to understand some of what I have experienced over the years and how it has brought me to the place I am today. Although incredible, astonishing things have happened to me – and I hope they will continue to happen as nothing gives me more joy – I am not a medium, a psychic, an angel lady or guru, and I certainly don't claim to have any special psychic 'gifts' or powers. I'm an ordinary 45-year-old mum with two children – my son is twelve and my daughter is eleven – and although some of the things I have encountered have been a direct result of my work as a spiritual writer, other things have simply happened. This has led me to believe that we are all born with Celtic souls, or the ability to see, hear and sense angels, and although many of us lose this sensitivity and open-mindedness as we grow older, there are ways to reawaken and reclaim it. A trip to Ireland may well be one of these ways, but it is by no means the only way. There are as many ways to reconnect with the divine as there are stars in the sky. For some of us the journey may take place on foot, but for others it may be an inner journey through our dreams or sudden hunches or insights, whereas for others it may be through coincidences or angel signs or calling cards, or a sense of connection with a departed loved one. The possibilities are endless.

I guess what I am trying to say here is that by sharing some of my psychic journey with you – and what were sources of transformation for me – I hope you will understand that anyone, however self-doubting and whatever their age or background, can have the profound connection with angels that is their birthright.

The rest of this book is a collection of real-life stories sent to me by people whose lives have been touched and transformed by angels in some way or other. These people come from all walks of life. Some, but by no means all, had a deep faith in angels or were devoted to a particular religion, but others did not describe themselves as religious in any way. Like many people today they believed in something, but they were not sure what. And then there were those who before their encounter did not think they believed in anything at all. All this confirms once again that although celestial beings of light appear in all the world religions, you do not need to be religious to see angels. All you need is an open mind.

The first batch of stories will focus exclusively on stories from Irish people or people who have visited Ireland and been transformed by it in some way. In these chapters I will be drawing from Ireland's rich spiritual heritage to reveal the treasures hidden within your own soul. My aim is to lead you to a place where your heart can be healed and nourished; a place where you can meet your own guardian angel, and discover your own true soul friend, your *anam cara*.

Then the stories will move away from Ireland to the rest of the world so you can read experiences of other people with magical souls. You'll read accounts here about people encountering healing angels or beings of light that intervened during times of danger or crisis, or angels that spoke to them through children, animals, dreams, signs or spectacular coincidences. Some of these stories will strike you with their profoundness; others may make you shed a tear and a few may make you smile. Some will send shivers down your spine; others will astonish you or even stretch your belief, but let me assure you again that they are all, to the best of my knowledge, true. Although in some cases names and other personal details have been changed to protect identity, all of these stories are the real deal. They actually happened, and demonstrate the myriad different ways that heavenly encounters can inspire people's lives, and they all bring messages of comfort, love and hope from the other side. In addition, all the stories you will read are reproduced authentically. In other words, as few changes as possible have been made to the narrative in terms of style and content to ensure that what you are reading is again the real deal.

A number of anecdotes were sent to me in response to my previous angel books, and some were gathered by me during trips to Ireland, while others were collected over the twenty-odd years I have been writing features about the psychic world. Everyone who contributed to this book, either by getting in touch with me or allowing me to interview them, has touched me deeply with their honesty and openness. As always, I am incredibly indebted to everyone, and if you can't find your story here I am sorry, it is simply because I ran out of space to include it. I do feel so very privileged to be given your permission to share your experiences with a wider audience.

The power of belief

During the years I have been a paranormal writer I have lost count of the number of times people have told me that reports of angels can be explained perfectly rationally. That they are products of an overactive imagination is one of the most popular explanations. In the early days of my writing career I would try to do all I could to prove that angels were real. I would point out that angelic encounters have been reported in every culture for thousands of years and many of these encounters have remarkable similarities. I would argue that in a court of law an eyewitness account is taken as evidence. I would even try to show that from a quantum scientist's perspective angels are simply things we have yet to understand well enough. It did not take me long to realise that I was wasting my time because angels are invisible beings of spiritual light and if a person's mind and heart are closed to their existence their existence can never be proved. The proof of their existence is therefore a very personal thing.

Basically, it is all a question of personal faith, and to those who believe, because their lives have been touched by heaven or because they have an affinity with the message of hope angels are trying to bring, no proof is necessary because nothing will have more power than their belief. In some cases the conviction that angels are real can be sudden and dramatic, but in many cases the conviction appears to happen little by little – in the wonderment of nature, in sudden realisations and *déjà vu*, in intuitions, in dreams or happenstance coincidences. And this is, of course, where once again we can learn such a great deal from the Irish. Even those with just a single drop of Irish blood flowing through their veins tend to have a spiritual flame burning within them. It is a flame that burns deep within their souls, lighting the way, guiding them through life with joy and hope. and inspiring all those lucky enough to cross their path to also see the world through angel eyes, or at the very least open their hearts to the idea that heaven is real.

Whether you are Irish or not, whether you have had an angelic experience or not, I hope that reading these astonishing stories about people whose lives have been touched by heaven will remind you that you too are a spiritual being. We all have a spiritual flame, a Celtic soul, lighting the way for us inside our hearts. I hope these stories will encourage you to listen more to your heart and to live your life with an awareness of spirit. I hope they will make you laugh or cry, or move you in some way, because every time a person is touched by reading an angel story, angels fly closer to earth, bringing with them their pure unselfish love and peace.

So, if you feel ready, prepare to be astonished and inspired by the stories in this book. As with every angel book I have written, working on it has renewed and refreshed my connection to the world of spirit and opened my eyes to new and wonderful possibilities. It is my sincere wish that it will do the same for you by showing you that all over the world ordinary people can open their doors and their minds and hearts to their angels and experience the magic, hope, love and blessings they bring with them.

CHAPTER ONE

The Stranger Who Changed My Life

The Irish: be they kings or poets or farmers
They're a people of great worth.
They keep company with angels
And bring a bit of heaven here to earth.

Irish saying

When I started work on this book I did seriously wonder if I was the best person to write it.

I was suitable in the sense that I believe in an afterlife. I believe that loved ones watch over us from the other side and that guardian angels, or spiritual guides, walk with us through the journey of our life. I also believe that angels can manifest themselves in countless visible and invisible ways. They may appear as a feather, a puff of air, an invisible kiss, a song that speaks to your heart, a spellbinding coincidence, a mysterious scent, a flash of insight, or in other people who are consciously or unconsciously guided by those from a spiritual dimension.

1

But I was the wrong person in the sense that I'm not Irish and this is primarily a book about Irish spirituality. How could I write convincingly about Irish spirituality without Irish blood running through my veins? I don't have any Irish relatives and I have visited Ireland only a few times. But then, as time wore on, and I did more research and a lot of thinking, I realised that for a whole lot of reasons I might, after all, be the ideal person to write it. My journey towards this point began five years ago.

Is this it?

Five years ago I wasn't coping very well. The days would start early and then stretch on and on with endless chores and free-lance writing work that wasn't challenging or fulfilling. I was always busy, but apart from being there for my family, all the things I did felt so trivial and meaningless. Some days I would wake up feeling like a washing machine that had been stuffed with too many clothes. I was spinning round, but only just, and I might break down at any moment. I guess you could say that I was thinking, Is this it? Is this as good as it will ever get for me? Surely life has to be about more.

Deep down I knew that I really had nothing to be unhappy about, and that there were many people far worse off than me. After all, I had my health, a loving husband and two remarkable young children. We were by no means rich but we had a roof over our heads and enough to keep going. I really should have been counting my blessings but instead I was counting missed opportunities. I was forty years old and hadn't really made my mark on the world as I dreamed I would do when I was a child. I hadn't really made the world a better place, or found a cure for cancer, or won the Nobel Peace Prize. I'd done OK with my writing but I hadn't written a number one bestselling book. I hadn't started my own business or come up with an original idea. I was making progress with my psychic skills but I hadn't had any full-blown angel encounters. I wasn't earning a six-figure salary. With the years catching up on me it was becoming increasingly clear that my childhood hopes and dreams were going to remain just that – dreams. I wasn't ever going to be particularly talented or outstanding at anything.

Before, when I had faced disappointment or had my hopes dashed in some way, I had always comforted myself with the thought that maybe one day things would be better, but now, with my forty-first birthday fast approaching, the future no longer held any sense of possibility for me. I felt old and increasingly like a has-been: a has-been that never really was.

Sometimes I got so disappointed and angry with myself. I looked back at my life and saw only confusion and wrong turns. Oscar Wilde once said that youth is wasted on the young, and how I agreed with him. I longed to be able to turn back the clock and do things so differently. I thought about the wonderful opportunity life had offered me when, from a broken, poverty-stricken home, I defied all the odds and got into Cambridge, and how my lack of self-confidence had squandered that chance. I left with a degree, but with absolutely no sense of direction or purpose as far as my career was concerned. I thought about the jobs that I had had and how I'd failed to distinguish myself in any way. I thought about my relationships before marriage and regretted bitterly all the tears I had shed and all the time I had wasted stressing and obsessing over men who didn't value me. I thought about my friendships and how unfulfilling they had been because I'd never been able to stand up for myself. I thought about my mum and how I had not been there for her when she died. I thought about my children and berated myself for the bouts of depression I had suffered when each was born. I thought about my marriage and how by letting the children have centre stage I was putting my husband in the wings and how little he deserved that. I thought about myself as a mother and how little joy I seemed to be getting out of that. I'd look at other mothers all rosy-cheeked and laughing as they played with their children, while I often felt like a robot. I made sure my children wanted for nothing and I loved them with a passion, but sometimes my heart was not fully in it.

I think you get the picture. I was beating myself up for not being the kind of successful, charming, disciplined, clever, rich, accomplished, charismatic, slim and blissfully content yummy mummy I had always hoped I would be. I compared myself constantly to other women and always felt I was lacking in some respect. Slowly and gradually a black, impenetrable cloud of disappointment and disillusion was descending over me. There had been times in the past when I'd experienced similar black spells, but somehow this one felt more tragic and disappointing, because at my age and with the life experiences I had had I really, really, really should have known better. I was getting too old for such self-absorption and self-pity.

Here's an extract from my diary, written in April 2005. It pains and embarrasses me to include it here because it is so self-indulgent, but it really does capture the way I felt.

21 April 2005

How horrible do I feel today. Let me count the ways. Right up there are feelings of uselessness. Once again I have that feeling that everything I have done so far in my life means nothing and everything I do doesn't matter. I try to get down to my writing but no matter how hard I try to focus it is never good enough. Much worse, I feel like everybody knows what a failure I am and I feel so guilty for that because I know I should be more for them. I look at my untidy house and feel like a failure. I go over and over all the times I have let down my kids. I stopped breast-feeding my daughter too soon. I didn't play with my son enough. I feel like a failure as a mother. Then I look at myself in the mirror and wonder why on earth my husband stays with me. I'm getting wrinkles and losing my looks and I feel like a failure as a wife.

I've just dropped the kids off at school. It's only just after nine o'clock and I feel so tired. The day stretches ahead of me and it feels like an overwhelming thing. Just washing my hair this morning took it out of me. It's not just the physical tiredness, I could cope with that, it's the mental tiredness that knocks me sideways. My mind feels so sluggish. I can't think straight and even remembering the name of my children's teacher is difficult. I lost my temper this morning with the children too and I regret that. Sitting here now writing this I really feel they are better off without me.

The phone just rang. I know who it is. One of the mums from my son's school wants to know if he can come round to play this evening. I can't bear the thought of talking to her, and even though I know my son would love to go, I just can't face it right now. I feel so trapped, so worthless. Things are not going to get better now. Life is passing me by; I am existing, not living. Is this it?

It's a grim read, isn't it? In the months that followed things didn't get much better. I was plagued by insomnia, feelings of sudden panic and dread, and constant and unrelenting bouts of senseless crying. Some would say I was having a nervous breakdown. Doctors don't like using the term, but whatever it was called one thing was certain: I was very close to the edge. I'd spend hours and hours on the internet doing nothing productive but trying to trace sales of my books, or lack of them as the case may be. I started to get splitting headaches. Some days they were so bad I couldn't function properly. Eventually I went to a doctor. I was convinced I must have some kind of brain tumour. He referred me to an eye specialist. I had all the checks but the specialist could find nothing wrong with me, until he asked me how many hours I spent on the computer. When I told him that some days it was in the region of eight or so hours he told me that it was very important for me to cut down or at the very least make sure I took breaks every half an hour or so. I was developing a serious case of eye strain. I knew he was right but I was so addicted to working online, in fact doing everything online, I knew I wouldn't be able to kick the habit.

So I limped along for another few months with the only concession being that I started wearing spectacles for computers, driving and television. It did ease the headaches for a while, but it didn't ease my sense of incompleteness, of dissatisfaction.

And then overnight my headaches and sense of emptiness mysteriously vanished when out of the blue my first angel book hit number nine on the *Sunday Times* non-fiction paperback bestsellers list. Suddenly, I felt a sense of pride and elation. I walked on air for weeks. I started laughing again. I was a happier wife and mother. I got in touch with old friends. After years of trying to get an agent for my writing, one actually contacted me and the very real possibility that I could make a living out of my passion for writing reared its head. Emails and stories flooded in from excited readers of my book and I felt energised as never before with a sense of purpose and direction. My life mattered. It was clear my angels had a plan for me. This was the moment my life had been waiting for.

My new-found happiness didn't last very long though. Within three months I was on shaky ground again. Feelings of failure and worthlessness came back like rust and mould. I'd forgotten how draining they could be. On the outside things were going well, very well indeed. I had fulfilled a childhood dream of become a successful writer, but even that wasn't enough to keep my head above water. I craved more success and attention. My second angel book came out two months after the first one. Perhaps it was too soon for a second title to come out, and that may have been the reason for it not doing so well as the first, but whatever the reason it barely scraped into the top twenty.

My second book not generating as much interest or sales was a crushing blow. The heaviness was back. I got through the days by putting one foot in front of the other because I really didn't know what else to do, but at the same time I felt like I was going to fall apart at any second. I would wake up in the middle of the night and cry with disappointment. It was like someone had pulled a rug from underneath me. I didn't know what the hell was happening. The best way I can describe it is like being sucked into a vortex, like the Dementors draining their victims' souls in the *Harry Potter* novels. I didn't dare tell my husband or family what I was experiencing. I was too ashamed.

I'm hoping what I have written so far hasn't shocked you too much, especially if you have read some of my previous books and know that I have a deep and powerful belief in the world of spirit and have also said that this belief has saved my life many times over. The reason I am telling you now is because I think it is important for you to know that even though I believe angels are real this doesn't stop doubts, fears and uncertainties from rearing their ugly heads. I think this would be true of anyone who looks up to heaven for inspiration. Yes, there have been wonderful highs in my life – moments when heaven shone through and everything made absolute sense and I have been able to rise above material concerns – but there have also been some very terrible lows when I have felt trapped and disappointed with myself and my life. Moments when I couldn't go on, when everything I ever thought was true and gave me a sense of meaning and purpose still couldn't lift me up.

Even today I still have my anxieties and doubts, but the difference between now and five years ago is that I have finally learned how to cope with them in a way that uplifts and inspires me, rather than draining and exhausting me. I guess you could say I have at long last learned how to live in spirit; how to rise above the need for approval, worldly success and status and how to stop fear, self-doubt and self-absorption controlling me. It took me over forty-five years to get there, but it was well worth the wait.

There have been several key moments or turning points in my life but nothing as profound or utterly life-transforming as the one that took place during my first trip to Ireland in late 2006. I can honestly say that after that trip my life was never to be the same again. Before, I believed in angels, but I wasn't sure I could trust them to make me feel at peace with myself. I thought of life as something to be endured rather than enjoyed. I thought true happiness and fulfilment weren't possible in this life. But after that trip I finally learned to trust my angels with all my heart and only then did my life in spirit truly begin.

The stranger who spoke to my heart

It was a cold November morning when my plane landed at Dublin airport. There had been delays and I was feeling stressed as a busy day of radio interviews and a pre-recorded TV interview had been scheduled to promote one of my books. I was nonetheless relishing this interest from the media in my work and there was a flutter of excitement in my stomach. I hadn't felt so alive in years.

The day went really well. I thoroughly enjoyed every moment and was treated like royalty by the radio and TV stations. As I headed for the airport in my taxi, I felt that I had really come into my own. This was the life I wanted to lead. This was what I loved to do. I felt like I was somebody at last. I felt warm from the inside. I was glowing. After I had checked in at the airport I had a good hour and a half to wait until my flight back home, so I grabbed a coffee, found a quiet corner and started reading the newspaper. It was blissful to have this time to myself.

A few minutes later a woman came and sat beside me. At first she annoyed me slightly because I had less room to read my paper; little did I know that this woman was going to change my life for ever. Realising I was taking up too much of the seat I shuffled to one side and in the process knocked my coffee over, spilling hot liquid all over my trousers. It really hurt and I cursed out loud.

'Are you OK?' the woman asked, handing me a cotton hand-kerchief to dry myself. Her voice was rich and musical with an unmistakable Irish accent. I think she was older than me but there was something childlike about her. She was dressed in purple and yellow and her delicious perfume filled the air. She was the kind of person who could light up a room. The kind of person I always wished I could have been. I felt very boring dressed as I always did almost entirely in black. I'd started wearing black in my teens and try as I might to experiment with colour I always found myself going back to black.

10

Although my leg was soaked, I hadn't burned myself seriously and reassured the woman that I would be all right. She
wasn't convinced so I told her again that I would be fine. She
looked relieved and then startled me by asking if I was going
to or had just come from a funeral. I had no idea what she
was talking about and then the penny dropped. I was wearing
black and she assumed it was for a funeral. I laughed and told
her that this wasn't the case and that I had come for a series of
radio interviews for a recently published book. She smiled and
I thought she was going to ask me the title of the book, as most
people would, but instead she asked me if I had managed to
travel around Ireland while I was here.

'The thought did cross my mind,' I replied. 'I've often
wanted to travel around Ireland and . . .'

I never finished the sentence because I didn't know what else
to say. I had lived in the UK all my life and apart from the odd
holiday abroad and a two-year work assignment in the US had
never travelled far away from my home. Suddenly, my life felt
very small. The lady looked at me earnestly and asked me why I
didn't travel, if it was something I wanted to do. She reminded
me that I only had one life and she always thought it best to live
each day as if it were the only one.

Her words made me think about how I was living my life. I
wasn't really quite sure. I had a firm belief in the world of spirit
and the eternal power of love but this hadn't stopped feelings
of restlessness and dissatisfaction creeping up on me in recent
years. I found myself asking this woman if she ever worried
about the future, or the meaning of her life. Sometimes it is so

much easier to talk to a stranger, someone who knows nothing about you. She didn't reply. She just laughed and shrugged her shoulders, and as she did I felt a pang of envy. This woman was so carefree. Always a serious, rather earnest, nervous person, I don't think I had ever really been carefree in my life.

I think the woman sensed my distress and confusion because she then did something ridiculous but profound. She took back the handkerchief she had given me and turned it over. She pointed to the embroidery on the back of the handkerchief and remarked how messy it was. Then she turned it back over and pointed at the beautiful flowers the embroidery had created. 'That's how I cope with it,' she said. 'Life is messy like the back of this handkerchief, but then I turn it around and it all makes sense. I think somewhere, somehow, when things are turned around it must all make perfect sense, it must all fit into place to create something beautiful, even the things that feel wrong.'

There was no stopping me now. I hadn't been able to talk intimately like this to someone about what really mattered in life for years, certainly not since my mum had died. It felt so natural talking to this woman, even though I had no idea who she was. I found myself telling her about my recent bouts of depression. How I lived in fear of them striking at any time. How even when things were going right in my life I didn't feel safe and how I longed to feel safe, secure and certain of who I was and what my life was all about.

'Safe!' she chuckled. 'Why would you want safe? There is nothing in this life or even the next that is safe. Everything is a risk and that is what makes everything so wonderful. Not knowing how things will turn out or why they happen. If you knew everything that would happen to you think how limiting that would be. If you knew the reason why bad things happen that would numb you to the suffering of everyone and everything. I wouldn't want to live in a world like that where nobody reached out to anybody else, would you? Not knowing is far better.'

There were a few moments of silence as I tried to take in what she was saying. Then she got up and looked right into my eyes.

'You know, a ship is safe in a harbour, a bird in a cage, a tiger in a zoo, but that is not where they are meant to be.'

There was a flight announcement and we both paused and turned away from each other to try and hear what was being said.

'I'm going now,' she said. 'It was good talking to you, Theresa.'

As if in a daze I got up and watched her walk away. I sat down and realised I didn't even know her name and I didn't recall telling her mine. I looked ahead to see if I could call out to her but she was nowhere. I looked all around me. This woman had just disappeared. I also noticed that my leg was completely dry and the cup of steaming coffee I thought had been knocked on the floor was still sitting on the bench beside me. I picked it up and it was half full. I rubbed my eyes. Was it possible? I could scarcely contain my excitement. Had I imagined the woman or fallen asleep and dreamed her? Or had I actually met my guardian angel right here at Dublin airport?

On the flight back I couldn't stop thinking about my surreal conversation. I fell into a deep sleep and dreamt about tigers roaming free and ships on stormy seas. I awoke with a gnawing feeling in the pit of my stomach. Whether she was a guardian angel or not, one thing was certain: I had felt incredibly close to this woman and been able to open up to her and tell her things I would not normally have shared with anyone because we had talked on a soul level. She had not been interested in my books or outward appearance but in what was going on inside me – in who I really was. It was a revelation and, guardian angel or not, the impact on my life was nothing short of angelic.

It suddenly became clear to me in a 'light-bulb moment' that the reason for my unhappiness, my constant feelings of disappointment and dissatisfaction, was that my success in writing was profoundly affecting my view of myself – my world was still governed by how much others valued me. I was still judging my worth on how the world regarded me, or how I compared to others in terms of looks and wealth and status, and that was why my life kept fluctuating between highs and lows.

I was obsessed with what I thought I wanted rather than what I really needed. I was neglecting my soul and this was making me feel distressed and destructively perfectionist and discontented. Not to mention that my focus on status and success was damaging my emotional health and destroying my peace of mind. I had got so caught up in material concerns that I had forgotten the real meaning of life.

How on earth had I let that happen? How on earth had I forgotten the transformative and redemptive power of love and wonder? These feelings add sparkle to life and are heaven-sent. They give life its beauty and interest. When they are repressed, life can be deadly empty and unfulfilling. So, if I wanted to escape those feelings of inner emptiness I needed to open my heart and learn to see magic in the everyday. I needed to get in touch with my heaven-sent emotions. I had to stop letting my head rule my heart. It was time for me to trust my heart again. It was time for me to understand – truly understand – that true happiness is an internal creation and not one that can ever be created by the outside world. Success as a writer was never, ever going to bring me true happiness. Being the perfect mother and wife was never going to completely fulfil me. True fulfilment could only come from within by connecting with my inner angel.

It was all so obvious – so simple – I could not believe I had been so blinkered all these years. Sure, I had had moments of lucidity, but always in the background, this fear of not being good enough, rich enough, clever enough or successful enough had made me look outside myself for answers, for approval and for a sense of self-worth, when all along all I needed to do was look deep within. My excessive concentration on my work, my achievements or having so-called psychic powers was actually leading me away from the love within me. I did not need to look around me for love. I needed to be still and find it within. I did not need to look around me to find angels. I needed to discover my angels within. Only when I could do that would there be no more fear or feelings of insecurity and incompleteness.

Trouble was, looking within always felt frightening – I might not like what I saw. Perhaps I wasn't as spiritual, loving and self-less as I thought I should be. Perhaps I didn't want to confront the darker aspects of my personality like this. I was running away from my dark side, but what my trip to Ireland taught me was that by refusing to look within I was also running away from the light within me. It was somehow easier to hide behind my doubts and fears, uncertainties and addictions because they gave me an excuse not to shine. I was afraid of discovering my true power. What might I do with it?

I'm going to quote something wonderful and fairly well-known now that says what I am trying to articulate far better than I ever could:

'Our deepest fear is not that we are inadequate. Our deepest fear is that we are powerful beyond measure. It is our light, not our darkness, that most frightens us. We ask ourselves, "Who am I to be brilliant, gorgeous, talented, fabulous?" Actually, who are you not to be?

You are a child of God. Your playing small does not serve the world. There is nothing enlightened about shrinking so that other people won't feel insecure around you. We are all meant to shine, as children do. We were born to make manifest the glory of God that is within us. It's not just in some of us; it's in everyone. And as we let our own light shine, we unconsciously give other people permission to do the same. As we are liberated from our own fear, our presence automatically liberates others.'

Marianne Williamson, *A Return to Love*

To return to my meeting with that mysterious lady in Ireland, did I meet my guardian angel that day? Yes, I believe I did and it has never ceased to fascinate me that the guise chosen by heaven was that of an Irishwoman. And when I put that meeting together with all that I was learning about ancient Celtic spirituality in my research work, I felt shivers down my spine. I was being sent unmistakable angel calling cards and I would be a fool to ignore them.

Six months later I followed the lady's advice and booked a short break in Ireland for a week. It was to be the first of many because during that week I found out exactly why she had urged me to visit. If there is any place on earth where you might feel the closeness of angels it is Ireland. The ancient Celtic reverence for the spirit in all things survives today – a vibrant legacy of spiritual wisdom quite unique in the Western world. There is so much for us all to learn from it.

So what can Celtic spirituality teach us today?

I'll explain in more detail as the book progresses but for now one of the first and most important things we can learn is that happiness cannot ever be found in the external. If we try to find happiness outside ourselves our inner emptiness will haunt us. We will become depressed and anxious and unfulfilled if we do not articulate our spiritual needs.

We can also learn the importance of savouring every precious moment of our lives. The Celtic mind does not separate human from divine or what is outside from what is within us. In other words, heaven is not some place out there, waiting for us when we pass over. It is waiting for us to discover, here and now within and around us.

As well as underlining the vital significance and transformative power of love, Celtic wisdom is also full of a sense of belonging and immediacy. It glorifies the light and this could well be why it is enjoying a surge of popularity today. With more and more people disillusioned with religion and science and the advance of materialism, feelings of loss and emptiness are rampant. We urgently need to rediscover light and to find a place where our souls can feel a sense of belonging and a sense of completeness again. And by so doing we can rediscover how to simply be, to see magic and possibility in the here and now, something we all find harder and harder as worries and cares pile up. Living in the moment, letting the past go and grudges die is a happy way to live. We can also learn to love unconditionally, not just others but more importantly ourselves; to forgive ourselves for mistakes made.

We can discover the rich rewards of opening our minds and filling them with new thoughts and ideas and living each new day with passion. No matter whether we succeed or fail at a particular task or project it is all a learning experience, and if we put time and effort into something we love we will always find success because we know deep down in our souls that we gave it everything we could.

Perhaps most significant of all, especially as far as this book is concerned, is that in the Celtic tradition there is no clear division between this world and the next and the presence of angels is accepted as an everyday reality. The importance of laughter and lightness when it comes to spiritual matters is also a characteristic. We are all in danger of letting life's worries and cares weigh us down, but it doesn't have to be that way. As I discovered firsthand on my trips to Ireland it is possible to keep in touch with spirit without being weighed down with seriousness.

Years ago when I used to regularly attend spiritual courses, workshops and lectures, one thing that always depressed me a little was the heaviness and seriousness of everyone involved. I used to feel the same when I attended religious services, especially when reciting prayers in school assemblies. Everyone would bow their heads and mumble words without feeling or thought, even when the words were beautiful. On one yoga retreat I don't think I heard anyone laugh for a whole ten days. It always felt wrong to me and also made me think that perhaps I was approaching my spiritual development with far too heavy a hand. My research on angels over in Ireland has shown me that spirituality and laughter can go hand in hand. Almost all the people I spoke to, just like the mysterious lady I met at Dublin airport, had that wonderful twinkle in their eyes when they spoke to me – even when they spoke of the most profound and sometimes heartbreaking things. They taught me that for many years I had been far too intense and serious in my approach to matters spiritual. I didn't realise that when we laugh and experience joy we are closer than ever to our angels.

Perhaps because we are dependent on gravity to keep us grounded on earth we tend to become weighed down with the serious and heavy stuff, sometimes to the point of taking ourselves far too seriously. Angels are charged with important work – the spiritual tasks of courage, dedication, commitment, patience and education – but they carry them lightly, going about them with joy, wonder, freedom, openness, spontaneity and love. Remember that famous Chesterton saying that angels can fly because they take themselves lightly. This does not mean they lack gravitas, just that they complete serious tasks with a lightness of spirit that comes from complete trust in the power of love.

Staying light in spirit isn't always easy, especially when life burdens you down with pain and heartache, but life isn't easy and wasn't meant to be. If there were no problems and no heartaches, how could we learn and grow in spirit; how could we choose the light? But if we can face the challenges life throws at us with an open, trusting heart like the Celtic souls whose stories are in this book, our angels will stand by us and give us the courage, optimism, energy, joy and hope to pull through.

Never forget, the meaning of the word angel is 'messenger' and the messages they bring are always ones of comfort, reassurance and the knowledge that we are not alone in this life and the next. For those that believe – and there are many of us – just the thought of them is comforting and adds a sweetness and lightness to our lives.

Your Celtic pilgrimage begins

Many Irish people have always had an interest in angels, ever since they were taught about guardian angels as children, so their insights and their stories provide the perfect launching point to help us all learn how to connect with our own angels. That's why the next two chapters will try to take you on a mini guided tour of Irish spirituality and the deep-rooted belief in angels that is a prominent feature of it. You'll discover, as I have, that Ireland is a deeply spiritual place because the Irish people make it so. Every person, place and object is held in reverence as though everything were blessed. Punctuated throughout with real-life stories from Irish people, as well as visitors to Ireland, or those who are simply Irish at heart, you'll see that although being Irish, or visiting Ireland, isn't a prerequisite for seeing angels, it can certainly act as a catalyst.

I hope this book will one day inspire you to make a pilgrimage to Ireland, but having said this, please don't feel you need to dash off to Ireland right now. I would feel like I had failed if that were the message you took away with you. As I hope my story in this introduction has made clear, encouraging you to search outside yourself for answers is not the purpose of this book; its purpose is to encourage you to look deep within yourself for answers and all around you for angels. It may surprise you to discover that St Patrick himself, the saint most of us associate with all things Irish, was not in fact Irish. More about him later; I just mentioned him here to impress on you that you don't need to have Irish blood running in your veins to have a Celtic soul.

Remember, it is not who you are, where you were born, what you do, where you go, who you associate with or even what religion you adhere to that draws your angels closer to you.

Your angels can see beyond all that. Rather it is the ability to see magic within and around you, to love unconditionally, to have an open mind and to live every day with enthusiasm and a spirit of joy and adventure that can nurture and sustain the special bond between earth and the invisible world. And if you can find these qualities within you, you can rediscover your special bond with heaven, right here, right now – today, without travelling anywhere. You can rediscover your Celtic soul.

So, if you are ready, it is time now to begin your pilgrimage to Ireland to rediscover and reunite with your *anam cara*, your soul friend and your heart's desire. I promise you that making such a journey to feed your soul, whether by plane, on foot, or if that isn't possible in your heart, will transform your life for ever.

CHAPTER TWO

Anam Cara

May you have: a world of wishes at your command.
God and his angels close to hand. Friends and family
their love impart, and Irish blessings in your heart!

Irish blessing

Ireland has many names: the Emerald Isle, Eire, Erin, the Land of Saints or, my favourite, the Land of a Thousand Welcomes. But whatever name you give it one thing is undeniable: Ireland is a place of beauty, heart and, above all, spirit.

Since ancient times Ireland has been renowned as a land of spirit; a land where the veil between this world and the next was said to be very thin. And to this day Ireland is still regarded as a beacon of spiritual wisdom. Special trips and pilgrimages are planned for ancient Irish holidays. Tourists flock to sacred sites and books on Irish spirituality lead the way. At a time when religion is losing its hold over the vast majority of people, the world still looks to Ireland to save its spiritual component. Indeed, Irish spirit is enjoying a major revival today with the huge popularity of Irish mystic and writer Lorna Byrne, a lady who sees spirits and angels playing a significant part.

But what makes Irish spirituality unique and wonderful – and ideal in my opinion as the launching pad for the current resurgence of interest in angels – is that with the exception of the tragic war in the North there are rarely any divisions between different layers of spiritual experience. Instead, history and belief systems flow into one another, assimilating and adapting to each other with remarkable tolerance and understanding, making Ireland's spirituality a living example of how differing religious visions can illuminate and enliven one another. For instance, Irish Christian pilgrims in ancient times did not follow the usual pattern of condemning other beliefs as demonic. Instead they adopted a great deal of the ancient Celtic religion, bestowing their saints with traits of the old gods or transforming the old gods into supernatural guardians with the power to intervene in human affairs.

So too is the case with belief in angels. For, although many people associate angels with religion, they are truly non-denominational spiritual beings able to adapt and assimilate into any religious or belief system. An enlightening study, produced in 2002 by scholar Emma Heathcote-James from the UK, illustrates this point perfectly. The study highlighted the great range of people who said they had encountered an angel. Those who came forward included Christians, Muslims and Jews, but 30 per cent gave no religion and 10 per cent said they were agnostic. Heathcote-James's study shows clearly that if you have a religious viewpoint angels can slot into any belief system, but you can also walk with your heavenly guides if religion is not for you.

You see, it is possible to be spiritual without being religious. Before angels began to reveal themselves to me, I experimented with a number of different religions but although I found beauty in all of them, I never truly felt at home. This led to periods of great doubt and uncertainty when I wondered if there was a heaven, but what I didn't realise at the time was that I did believe in something. I just didn't understand what that something was because I was seeking its definition in established religion, when what I should have been doing was looking within. Over the years I have found my faith again and even though I am not religious I call myself spiritual, because at last I understand what I believe in – the invincible and immortal power of love and goodness revealed to me every day by the world of spirit all around and within me.

What I am talking about here is a sense of the spiritual power in everyone and everything that transcends religion, and this sense of divine transcendence and transparency is an overwhelming feature of Irish spirituality. There is an awareness of the extraordinary that permeates every aspect of life. The ordinary is to some extent extraordinary and the extraordinary is somehow to be expected. This existence is a glimpse of the afterlife, of a transcendent place. Heaven is not something that exists 'out there'. It is something that can be experienced right here and now, within and all around you, making wonder and surprise the order of the day.

I'm jumping ahead of myself here in my excitement. Time to go back to basics.

Who were the Celts?

Irish spirituality has its roots in the beliefs of the ancient Celts (pronounced *Kelts*). The Celts were a distinctive cultural group originally from Central Europe. They migrated to Ireland as well as parts of England, Scotland and Brittany in northern France around 500 BC after they had been driven out by the Romans. Irish Gaelic is the Celtic language.

Saint Patrick introduced the Irish Celts to Christianity around 430 AD and many Celts converted, recognising the similarity between their beliefs and those of the Christian faith, especially the existence of the afterlife. However, whether they converted or not, what remained most distinctive about the Celts was their awesome awareness of the presence of the divine all around them, within and without. In addition, in the Celtic world-view, the hidden world of angels was a natural and very real part of creation. Indeed, angels were considered more real because they were not limited by time and place and so these invisible beings were life companions and throughout their daily routines believers acknowledged the presence and sought the help of their angels. As pointed out previously, this unique spiritual perspective is enjoying a resurgence of popularity today among those drawn to belief in angels and, in my opinion, consciously or unconsciously, anyone drawn to the idea of beings of light guiding and inspiring us through this life and the next has a Celtic soul.

If you have Irish blood in your veins or are Scottish, Welsh or perhaps English, there is little doubt that you have Celtic roots. Europeans may also be surprised to find that they have distant Celtic roots, but a natural Celtic connection is certainly no precondition for spirituality. However, it is my firm belief that what makes the ancient Celts so appealing today to many people in search of a personal relationship with the divine that is not defined by religion or ritual is the fact that their relationship with heaven was powerful and intimate. The divine was immediately present to them in their daily lives, not just during times of inspiration, happiness and joy but also in daily routines and during times of pain and crisis. To this day people of Celtic origin are still recognised for the strength of their faith during both the good and the bad times.

For the ancient Celts this recognition of heaven's presence in every aspect of life was pivotal to their faith. Divine presence was alive in all creation and could be seen in every moment of life without the need for a church, ritual or intermediary. The immanent presence of heaven could also be recognised in their understanding of the life-changing power of love and companionship. And nowhere is this theme more beautifully expressed in Celtic tradition than in the idea of soul love: the old Gaelic term for this being *anam cara*.

Friend of your soul

Anam is the Gaelic word for soul and *cara* is the word for companion or friend, so in rough translation *anam cara* means soul love, soul kinship or friend of the soul. For the early Celts *anam cara* was the name given to a person who was a teacher or spiritual adviser. It was someone you could share your heart and soul and deepest desires with and there was an unbreakable and eternal bond between you.

Each and every one of us has a primal desire for an *anam cara*; someone who understands us completely and always has our best interests at heart. Someone you can trust with all your intimate secrets, hopes, desires and longings without judgement. When you feel understood and accepted in this way it feels like you belong or have come home. Many of us try to find this sense of identity and destiny in our relationships with others. We search high and low for our soul mates. Sometimes we strike lucky and do indeed find someone who seems to fulfil our every need, but even when that is the case there remains a sense of vulnerability and fear because people are not predictable and the spectre of a loved one's death or illness is always present.

Others, perhaps disillusioned by affairs of the heart, search for their *anam cara*, their sense of wholeness, in their work or career, but again, as I know from bitter experience, this is a fragile and unstable foundation to build your life and your happiness upon. Remember, no one ever says, 'I wish I had spent more time at the office' on their deathbed. Then there are those who find glimpses of hope in travel or in the accumulation of wealth or the acquisition of status, but again all these are never enough to truly satisfy your soul.

The only way to truly satisfy and illuminate your soul is in the *anam cara* experience and by that I mean looking within yourself for a sense of belonging, magic and destiny. The *anam cara* experience is heaven's gift to us. Many of us have an aspiring angel hidden within of whom we are truly unaware and this lack of awareness creates feelings of depression, longing and purposelessness that you may find hard to articulate or express. Sometimes tragic or dramatic life events such as the loss of a loved one, illness, job loss, divorce or dangerous situations can awaken a sense of divine presence within us, but it doesn't have to be that way. Our souls can find a sense of belonging in the everyday and the ordinary and this again is where Celtic tradition can teach us so much.

In Celtic tradition the concept of *anam cara* was not considered to be an abstract ideal. It was a soul kinship that was very much alive and present and always relevant and possible. It was a way of living and experiencing the world that brought true and lasting transformation and healing from the inside out because of the reassurance it offered that however difficult life gets we are never alone.

It is ironic that in today's world where we have never been better connected due to the astonishing advances in computers, media and technology, so many of us still feel alienated and alone. Millions of us claim to have hundreds of virtual 'friends' on online social networks, but the fact that the internet is replacing human interaction makes life feel ever more anonymous and isolating. True intimacy is a divine experience and something that cannot be found online or indeed through any human notion of relationship. True intimacy can only ever be found within our souls because true intimacy is sacred.

The Celtic tradition recognises the divine possibility that exists within each person in its everyday language. There is no word for 'hello' in Gaelic. Other people are greeted with the following blessing:

Dia dhuit –
Heaven be with you

When you leave a person there is no goodbye either but:

Go geumhdai Dia thu or *go gcoinne Dia thu* –
Heaven go with or protect you.

Indeed, throughout the Gaelic language there is this theme of divine presence in others. Even strangers are said to bring the 'blessing of heaven' with them. All this isn't to say that you can't find fulfilment in human encounters. It is a beautiful thing when two people love each other, and intimacy between friends and family has a divine honesty and clarity. But when two people unite in some way there is always a third and more powerful force at work binding them together, and if that relationship is to survive and thrive this spiritual force needs to be acknowledged. In other words, you can never truly and deeply love another person unless you are also actively working on the spiritual task of looking within for answers and beginning to learn to love yourself.

If you want to know what love is you don't need to look outside yourself and this is not selfish or narcissistic, it is a sacred calling – indeed, the very meaning of your life. You shouldn't try to force yourself if there are aspects of your personality you feel uncomfortable with, you should simply ask your guardian angel within – your *anam cara* – to welcome love into your heart so that bitterness, hardness, loneliness, fear and guilt can flow away. Whenever you get a moment to yourself just think about your guardian angel within, just focus on the potential for love and goodness inside your soul. One of the most productive times to do this is just before you go to sleep because when you sleep, it is often said, the angels have conversations with our souls.

You see, your only purpose in life is to discover love within and around you and to learn to accept and give love. Once you can welcome love into your soul you become strong and independent. You can love others not out of need or a sense of incompleteness or the need for affirmation but because you want to, because you feel free inside yourself first. It's been said many times over but love is the only thing that can ever truly set you free and allow you to be yourself. Your angel friends within and around you want you to retain your individuality. They want to give your soul room to express itself.

In the Celtic tradition there is an enchanting concept that if there is love within you it should be shared with others, and if you give love in this way it will come back to you countless times over. In other words, the more love and goodness you give or send to yourself and others, the more love you will discover all around you. I can think of no better place than here to include this traditional Irish friendship blessing. I first came across it – and indeed the beautiful concept of *anam cara* – in a wonderfully illuminating, divinely inspired and internationally bestselling book by the late John O'Donohue entitled *Anam Cara: Spiritual Wisdom from the Celtic World* (1997), and if you want to explore the spiritual ideal of *anam cara* further than this brief introduction, I highly recommend it.

Blessings to you.
May you be blessed with good friends.
May you be a good friend to yourself.
May you be able to journey to that place in your soul
Where there is great love, warmth, feeling and forgiveness.
May this change you.
May it transfigure that which is negative, distant or cold in you.
May you be brought into the real passion, kinship and affinity of
belonging.
May you treasure your friends.
May you be good to them and may you be there for them.
May they bring you all the blessings, challenges, truth and light
that you need on your journey.
May you never be isolated.
May you always be in the gentle nest of belonging with your
anam cara (soul friend).

Another distinguishing characteristic of Celtic spirituality is the prevailing awareness of the reality of the unseen world and of life after death. As mentioned earlier everything the Celts saw, heard, felt, tasted, touched or smelled could link them to the divine because the divine exists both on earth and in the invisible world of spirit. Just as heaven was real and everywhere, spirits and angels were also real and everywhere. Once again we can learn so very much from this Celtic way of knowing.

There is a great deal of scepticism and cynicism these days about things which science and logic cannot explain, and while the search for proof and evidence is frequently necessary and vital, there are also times when we need to step back and think about why there is such a need to explain every aspect of our lives rationally. Supernatural experiences can only ever be truly validated by faith because true faith requires us to accept that life is a mystery. The existence of heaven, for instance, will never be scientifically validated and most of what we know about it comes from witness statements and personal experiences. Belief in heaven originates in our hearts and not in our minds. Think about all the truly magical moments in your life. Were these moments we felt with our senses, or were they moments we felt in our hearts? Were these moments we observed or moments revealed from within? This world of inner perception is where both angels and the spirits of the dead dwell.

If you have lost a loved one the chances are you have sensed their presence within and around you. Like the angel within, those we have loved and lost also live within us. The Celts had a keen sense of the closeness of death and absolutely no doubt that there was life beyond death. The dead were living in spirit, and in death connections to this world were not destroyed but consolidated. Indeed, the Celtic tradition regarded death not as a terrible event but as a miraculous journey, because a person was returning to a place where no pain, loneliness, fear, failure or sorrow could ever hurt them again. It was a place where their inner angel could be set free and where they came face to face with the divine that always lived within them.

To risk repeating myself there is so much we can learn today from this approach to death. If you live your life to the full and find ways to connect to your angel within, death can never be something that is to be feared. It becomes instead the moment when you are released fully into the world of spirit. The soul is released from the limitations of the physical and the burdens of space and time to find its home in spirit. If you think of death not as the end but as a new beginning, this life is full of possibilities to awaken your spirit as you become aware of the treasures hidden within you and around you in the unseen world. Becoming spiritual and discovering life eternal is therefore about developing a sense of the depth and richness of the invisible world within you.

I'm aware this has been quite a deep and intense introduction to basic themes in Celtic spirituality – and there is a lot to digest – but I felt it was important to set the scene for the stories that follow. The accounts here are from Irish people I have met or been in correspondence with whose lives have been healed by their belief and trust in angels, within and around them. In different ways each one of them illustrates this sense of inner completeness, inner freedom and of love within and the love revealed everywhere that I have tried to articulate in this chapter. As you read, notice how they all found a way to rediscover and awaken their *anam cara*, their aspiring angel within and around them, and how this spiritual awakening quite literally transformed their lives.

I'm going to begin with this astonishing story sent to me by a lady called Brigid.

Lost in translation

I was born into a deeply religious Irish family but I never really connected with that side of life. As soon as I got my qualifications and was old enough to look after myself I left Ireland and my family and went to live in London. I even started having elocution lessons to try and lose my accent, so anxious was I to reinvent myself and find out who I really was. Five years after moving to London I thought my life was pretty darn good. I had a boyfriend who adored me and a job I loved. My sisters would often write to me and ask me to come home and visit but I always had an excuse. As I said, I needed to break free and I didn't believe in angels or life in spirit or anything like that until I had a brush with death.

It happened three years ago and I can't remember everything but I do remember walking home one night from the Tube and then this screech of metal. It all went black after that but what I know now is that a car mounted the kerb and crashed into me. I lost consciousness instantly and the next thing I remember is waking up in hospital.

I woke up in an emergency ward room and saw four nurses and doctors wearing pale blue. My throat was incredibly dry but I had this overwhelming need to say something to them. I asked them to take care of me and they nodded and smiled. One of the nurses, a woman with stunning green eyes, put her hand to my cheek and gently stroked it. I can't remember much more after that, just brief moments when I woke up and saw medical teams around me. I didn't fully regain consciousness until a few days later.

When I eventually woke up I saw my partner and my sisters sitting beside my bed. My mum was holding my hand. A doctor came in, followed by four nurses. They were the same ones I had seen before. I knew these people had saved my life and later when my partner and family left the room to take a break I had a chance to talk to the nurse with green eyes. She told me that I had had a lucky escape and apart from bumps and bruises I was going to be fine. It had been touch-and-go for a while though as I had sustained a head injury and doctors had needed to make sure I would not relapse. I thanked her again from the bottom of my heart and then she said the strangest thing. She asked me how often I spoke Gaelic. I told her that I could not speak a word of Gaelic and she looked as shocked as I did and went out of the room. Minutes later she was back with my doctor.

My doctor explained to me that when I had drifted in and out of consciousness I had been speaking in a different language. Nobody at first could understand it but a recording was made and I had been speaking Gaelic. Over and over again I had said the words '*shabhail dom*', which shakily translated means 'save me'.

Now I remember asking the nurse to help me when I came into hospital but I certainly don't remember saying it in Gaelic! I can honestly swear to you that I have never spoken Gaelic in my life. Everyone, myself included, was mystified and inspired by what had happened to me. It seems that in my deepest hour of need I had gone right back to my Celtic roots. How was that possible?

As I said, this all happened a few years ago now, and I often find myself thinking about what happened. I think about the miracle of my life being saved and the strange phenomenon of me speaking Gaelic when my life hung in the balance. It took me a while to understand the profound significance of it all, but it is my firm belief today that I was being sent a clear and powerful message from the angel within me and from the angels around me. I haven't moved back to Ireland but I've retained my Irish accent and am proud of my roots. I know who I am today. I'm not running away from myself anymore. I also know without doubt that there is more to this life than meets the eye. Something incredible happened to me in that hospital and it has convinced me that life in spirit is as real as this life on earth. Please go ahead and share my experience with anyone who will listen. I'd like to think it might go some way to transforming other people's lives in the same way it has transformed mine.

Brigid's story can teach us a lot about being true to who we are. It is the same with life in spirit. We may try to deny or run away from our spiritual roots but sooner or later something magical happens that gives us pause for thought.

Let's move forward now with this account from a gentleman called Ryan.

Moving forward

Last year I had an affair. My wife knew nothing about it and my lover knew nothing about my wife. I'm not going into the details but it started at work and I found myself leading a double life. The thing was, I couldn't decide what to do. I cared about them both and a part of me enjoyed the secrecy of it all, but then things took a dramatic turn when my wife told me she was pregnant. I actually had to sit down when she told me. I almost fainted. We hadn't planned on having children for a few more years. My wife is a devout Catholic so I knew she was going to keep the baby. I knew I was going to become a father. I knew I had to end my affair. I knew I had to tell my wife I had been unfaithful.

It took a week or so for me to gather enough courage but eventually I told my wife. She took it really badly and told me she never wanted to see me again. I don't blame her. I had been really selfish and out of control. She deserved better. I stopped seeing my lover too. It took breaking up with my wife for me to realise that she was the love of my life. Not knowing who to talk to or where to turn, as everyone – my parents, my in-laws, my brothers – was angry with me, I decided to get away for a week to clear my head. I rented a cottage in Moveen, County Clare, close by the sea. My parents had taken me there for holidays when I was a child and I knew it well.

When I arrived, at first the clear air did do me a power of good. I felt calmer, but after a few hours I started to feel really bad. I thought about the way my first child was conceived and how I could never make that right. I thought about my wife and the tears she must be shedding. I thought about my parents and how disappointed they must be with me. Everything felt bad and I knew it was time for me to leave. I thought about moving abroad and making a fresh start. I clearly wasn't wanted back home. I didn't have a home anymore.

So there I was in my cottage feeling alone and scared and guilty and ready to run away. Even though it was late spring it was pretty cold inside the cottage and I started to shiver. Then I felt this warmth all over my body. There wasn't any sun shining through the window. It felt like someone was placing a blanket around me. It was so comforting. Then I felt a gentle weight on my shoulders like someone was placing their hands on them. It felt like the comforting touch of a friend, even though there was nobody there. It felt like it was someone who wasn't giving me advice or telling me that things would turn out all right, because clearly that wasn't going to happen, but someone who was letting me know they were there for me. Something else happened too. I started to feel more in control. I started to think about what I had done and understand why I had done it. Mum had warned me that I was too young to get married – I married at nineteen – and she had been proved right. I also realised that running away was not and never would be the answer. I needed to face up to whatever I had done and do all I could to put it right.

So after my week-long break I returned to my wife and told her that I could not expect her to ever forgive me but I wanted to be there for our child. I also told her I was going to move out and rent a flat close by. And that is what I have done. My wife and I are still living apart but we are head-over-heels in love with our daughter, Clara. I couldn't imagine life without my beautiful daughter and I have my angel to thank for that. I am convinced my angel helped me make sensible grown-up decisions during that week in the cottage. Like a friend who tells you that you've messed things up but they are there for you if you need them, my angel helped me face up to my problems instead of running away from them. You could say my angel helped me grow up.

I guess the moral of Ryan's story is that to be human is to get things wrong, but however badly you mess up, however many mistakes you make, your guardian angel, like a true and devoted friend who loves you unconditionally, will never desert you. Your angel will be there to give you the strength to move forward, however tough that may feel at the time and however much you feel like crawling into a shell.

I think this next story will both fascinate and inspire. It was sent to me by a lady called Mary.

The go-between

When I first met Michael it was love at first sight, for me at least. He was gorgeous, intelligent and we had so much in common: our devotion to Ireland, our love of music and our passion for walking. We started dating and after six months he proposed and we got engaged. I couldn't have been happier, but then another six months passed and then another and then another and we were soon approaching four years of engagement. Every time I broached the subject of setting a marriage date Michael had some excuse or other – his company in Belfast was going through too many changes; his brother who lived in Australia wouldn't be able to fly over; he wanted to save more money. If there was an excuse to be made he made it until finally I ran out of patience. I knew he loved me. We'd been dating five years and we still laughed together and had a brilliant connection. So why didn't he want to put a wedding ring on my finger?

A lot of my friends told me I should threaten to leave him; put him on the spot. I was approaching my thirtieth birthday and I really needed to know if we had a future together or not. Some days I thought I should leave him; shock him into making a decision. Other days I thought I should give him the time he needed. The love we had for each other was worth waiting for. After several months of this indecision my frustration finally got the better of my understanding. I packed my bags, wrote Michael a letter explaining my reasons for doing so and moved back home with my mum.

It was an agonising thing to do, leaving someone you have such a strong connection with, but I knew I couldn't go on anymore with the indecision. He had to decide if he wanted to spend the rest of his life with me. If there were any doubts it was better we went our separate ways now before it was too late, so at least we could both have second chances at happiness. I thought he would call right away, at least talk to me, but days melted into weeks and it soon became clear that our relationship was over. My heart was ripped apart and on many occasions I thought about calling him or accidentally bumping into him on his way to work, but I stayed strong. At night I would cry my heart out. I missed him so very much and I would hug my pillow until I fell asleep. I simply did not understand how someone could turn their back on happiness as he had done. I longed for answers and one night about three weeks after I left, I got them.

I fell into a deep sleep and then I woke up in the middle of the night. I say I woke up but I now realise I woke up in a dream because I also knew I was asleep. In my dream I saw this woman and she was the spitting image of Michael – same eyes, same hair colour, same face and same smile. I knew she was his mother. Michael had never wanted to speak about his mother. All I knew was that she had left him when he was very young. In my vision Michael's mother came right up to me and gently touched my cheek. She told me to stay strong and to keep trusting my heart. She knew her son and she knew he loved me.

The next morning when I woke up I felt calmer than I had done in weeks. I still missed Michael but I didn't have that empty, incomplete feeling anymore. I knew it was time to stop weeping and wailing and get on with my life. If Michael wanted to return to me he would, but if he didn't then I wasn't going to fall apart. I could cope without him if I had to. I would rather not but you can't force someone to love you and commit to you if they are uncertain or not ready.

You aren't going to believe this, Theresa, but that very morning on my way to work I bumped into Michael! It was no accident though. He told me he wanted to see me and had done a lot of thinking. He wanted to marry me. I just could not believe it. I had let him go and now he had come back to me.

Michael and I married a year later and we have been married fifteen years now and over time he told me all about his mother. She hadn't left him when he was young, she had died giving birth to him. It was something his father couldn't cope with and that is why Michael had ended up in foster care at the age of five. When I told Michael about my night vision he was bewildered but incredibly moved. Was it possible that his mother had reached out to me to let me know that she wanted us to be together? Did she do all she could to make sure that her son would spend the rest of his life with someone who loved him enough to let him go?

This next contributor did not leave her name but as you can see from her story, Ireland is her spiritual home.

Fear of flying

I'm one of life's worriers. I worry about everyone and everything and for many years I've suffered from borderline obsessive compulsive disorder. Some days I'm better than others and it was on one of those days that I agreed to go on a short holiday to Ireland with an old friend. It sounded like a good idea at the time but as the days approached I started to worry more and more. I'm not good with flying and I worried that being out of my comfort zone might be all too much.

Anyway, I did manage to conquer my fears and go on the trip. By day three, though, I was longing to go home; I just could not relax and enjoy anything. My friend was in raptures about the sights and sounds of Ireland; all I could think about was whether my house was safe and secure.

On day four of our break, a trip to Blarney Castle, located near the city of Cork, was planned. I just wanted to get it over with as it was the last day before we were due to fly back. On the coach my friend chattered endlessly about the legends surrounding Blarney, but I didn't pay much attention. When we got there I felt even more out of sorts as the castle was mostly in ruins and not much to look at in my opinion. Then we had to walk up a seemingly endless, narrow and steep staircase. I'm not good with heights but my friend made me go up with her. When we got to the top of what must have been about eighty steps the tour guide seemed to want each one of us to lie down, grab some railings and kiss a stone. The guide said that according to tradition anyone who did so would receive the gift of eloquence.

I don't know what came over me but I found myself going along with it. As I said, I'm scared of heights so this was out of character for me, but I was swept along by the moment. When it came to my turn I had to grab some railings, lower myself a few feet and kiss the Blarney Stone on the parapet. There was a small grate between me and the tour guide holding me, but it was pretty stomach-churning. When I had kissed the stone I felt a rush of excitement and energy spin through me. I stepped back and took a look at the breathtaking view from atop the castle and it was like I saw it with new eyes. For the last few days I'd seen lots of Irish countryside but it had not spoken to me. I can only say I saw the beauty for the first time. Excitedly, I started to tell my friend all the wonderful things I could see. I think she was a bit taken aback as I had barely spoken two words the whole day.

Something else happened after my trip to Blarney. I felt more relaxed and content in my own skin. I didn't stop worrying altogether but I did stop worry taking over my life. It was the most wonderful vacation; truly life-changing.

Theresa, I don't know if kissing the stone was the catalyst for me or whether it was a combination of friendship, time out and beautiful countryside, but ever since, I have returned to Ireland time and time again for inspiration. When I'm there I feel like I can fly. Please feel free to use my story. I know it isn't about angels but perhaps I met my angel on top of a castle as you mention in your books that angels can reveal themselves in the most surprising and unexpected of ways.

No name was left for this next account either but again it is clear that it is written by someone with Irish blood in their veins.

Drunk in spirit

I read your angel book with interest and was particularly interested in the sections where you talk about angels revealing themselves in deeply personal ways.

I haven't seen angels as such but I have the good fortune to have been born and bred in Ireland. I never feel quite at home or as peaceful and inspired anywhere else. I don't know whether it is the music, the magnificent countryside, the endless stone walls that define the country, the road signs that seem to be designed to confuse, the castles, the refreshing rain and bracing winds or the busy streets with friendly faces stepping in time to the fiddle players. Its spirits warm my heart and its storytellers and musicians warm my soul. You see, even talking about Ireland makes me sound far more inspired than I am.

I'm not sure what you feel about the idea of a place offering you glimpses of heaven but I just wanted to share my thoughts.

This next letter was sent to me from Ireland by Valerie. I'm including it here because it shows her belief in a higher power to save, guide and inspire her life from childhood onwards, and such powerful belief is a defining characteristic of all the letters I receive from my Irish readers.

Day by day

This morning I woke up with the thought of writing you this letter. I feel compelled to because all through my life things have happened to me and I have always believed there is a heaven although I haven't been to church for a few years, maybe more.

One particularly memorable episode happened when I was fourteen years old. My family were all at the seaside and we were playing in a rock pool that was quite deep. At the side of the pool my father was throwing a ball for me and my two sisters to catch. My foot caught on a stone and I tripped. I could not swim and my father was fully dressed and could not swim either. I went down underwater. My sisters tried to pull me up. When I was going down for the third time I started feeling peaceful and calm and I could see through the murky water all the bubbles rising to the surface, but as I was looking up with my hand raised, instead of sinking further it was as if I was being lifted up or pushed up by something and this enabled my sister to reach me and pull me out. I could have died that day . . .

Another strange but inspiring experience happened when I was at art college. My sister's little boy, who was four years old, was really ill with cancer. He was taken to the Royal Victoria Hospital in Belfast where I was able to go and visit him. Unfortunately, there was nothing they could do for him so he was sent home. He died at that young age but before he did he told us he was not afraid to die and he talked about going to heaven. We were amazed that he knew so much. Anyway, his coffin was put upstairs and I went up to see him and placed a necklace with a cross on his coffin. My sister then took me downstairs. After a short while I had to go to the toilet which meant I had to go upstairs again and as I was making my way back down the stairs I swear I heard angels singing from the room he was in and it gave me such a comforting feeling . . .

Valerie went on to narrate other extraordinary incidents in her life when she feels an angel was on her shoulder and then she told me about some more recent experiences.

. . . The last four years have been very hard. My father passed away with cancer and my mother was so ill with lots of problems health-wise and she too passed away this year, in January. We almost lost her a couple of times when she was in hospital. My sister and I were in the coronary care unit and we noticed that mum was talking about some strange things. It was as if she was saying her goodbyes to everyone. She also started to talk about a bright light and seeing my dad and granny. She then tried to get up off the bed and reach up for something. When we asked her what she was trying to do she said it was time for me and my sister to leave the room but that we were to be sure to get the nurse. It felt so strange, the feeling that you get inside when you think that this is the end.

Since my mother's passing things have been happening in my house and in my dreams. One night I was on my own in the living room. It was around midnight and I had the television on. I decided to turn it onto the music channel Magic FM. I stood up in the dark and started to dance slowly by myself. I closed my eyes and there was my mother standing with her arms out as if she wanted to waltz with me. I danced around holding out my hand as if I was dancing with her and she was smiling. Behind her I could see quite a dark shadow which something just told me was my father. I danced for around ten minutes and it was the most wonderful, comforting feeling.

There have been other reassuring signs too, and before I managed to post this letter my mum appeared again, this time in a dream. I was standing outside my mum's house and the house next door that used to be my uncle's (Mum's brother). Sadly he committed suicide a few years ago after a major depression. Mum never really got over this. Anyway, as I was saying, I was standing at the side of our house and I looked up at the sky and saw two dark clouds sort of clash together and there seemed to be a triangle of light. With this, I looked over to my uncle's house and my mother came out from where the back door was and walked around to the side of the house. She looked a lot younger, with brown, wavy hair, but she looked at me and started waving. She was really smiling and she shouted over to me and said, 'I've never been so happy.' I woke up in the morning and the first word that came into my head was my uncle's first name. I hadn't thought of him in years and then I smiled to myself as I realised Mum had finally met up with her brother.

It has felt really good writing all this down to send to you.

I'm glad Valerie's letter mentions dreams because if you have read any of my books you will know that I believe vivid dreams that stay in your mind for months, even years after you have had them, are true messages from heaven. Such dreams differ from symbolic dreams – which tend to be less vivid and are usually forgotten instantly on waking – and I often refer to them as 'night visions' rather than dreams. Many people, like Valerie, have written to me over the years to tell me about night visions they have had of departed loved ones. They often ask me if this was indeed a communication from the other side and I truly believe that this is what these dreams are.

Once again Celtic spirituality is a source of inspiration and guidance here, and if you ever read about the lives of Celtic saints – Saint Patrick in particular – you will see just how seriously the ancient Celts took their dreams as divine messages that needed to be remembered and understood. Dreams are an important topic, and we will return to them later, but for now bear in mind that the psychologist Carl Jung once described dreams as 'communication every night', and for me that description pretty much captures the otherworldly splendour and radiance of dreams. All we need to do is remember and understand the beauty and the mystery.

Moving on now, here is a letter sent to me by Arthur, who describes an incident that happened to him several years ago on world-famous O'Connell Street. When I first read it, I cried.

Seeing the light

I never thought I'd admit to this but I was once an alcoholic. In the summer of 2000 I lost my job and my wife of seven years left me. I thought I had nothing to live for except the bottle.

On the day my divorce papers came through I went to the off-licence and bought as many bottles of wine and gin and cans of beer as I could. On the way home, with the bottles and cans clinking in my bags, a cyclist flew past me and sprayed mud all over me. I lost my balance and fell to the side of the road onto my bags of drink. Several bottles broke and there was glass everywhere. I tried to salvage as much as I could, in the process cutting my fingers, but it was hopeless.

All of a sudden I felt as though something was pouring out of me through my head. The sensation was so great that I held my head in my hands. Then I heard a high-pitched sound in my ear and out of the corner of my eye I saw a little light – a small, very bright light that got larger and larger. I wasn't scared, just amazed. The light touched me above my heart. I jumped a little because I was startled. The place where I was touched was a warm spot that seemed to travel throughout my entire body. As the warmth spread, I lost my taste for alcohol.

To this day I am certain that an angel came to me that day. My life has changed. I've rebuilt it and I've been sober for eight years and counting. I've got a new job and a new partner and life couldn't be better. That experience changed my life. It was a miracle. I have told this story only to my closest friends. Some believe me while some do not, but this is definitely what happened.

At the time, I wrote back to Arthur to tell him that I most certainly believed him. I didn't hear back but, by a stunning coincidence, he got in touch with me while I was writing this book to tell me his faith burns as bright as ever and that he is now the proud father of a 3-year-old son called Conner – it was as close as he could get to O'Connell Street.

I'm going to continue here with this intriguing story sent to me by a lady called Caitlin. It certainly gave me a lot to think about when I read it and I hope it gives you pause for thought too.

The note

I was walking home one day and my head was the usual jumble of work and family. I'm a teacher – I've been teaching in Ireland for twenty years – and it was close to exam period, so there was so much to do. As I walked home the name of an old friend kept popping into my head. I'd been meaning to call her for months but had put it off because I was so busy. Suddenly, though, I had a sense of urgency and instead of calling her I just knew I had to actually call round. It was crazy, really, as I had mountains of paperwork to do before the next morning but instead I found myself running home and jumping into my car. My friend lives in Cookstown, so it took me a good while to get there in the rush hour. I tried calling her on the way but there was no answer.

When I arrived at her house I felt really stupid because there was no one home. I had come all this way for nothing. I waited a while and then wrote a note saying I had been in the area and hoped to catch up. I dated the note and put a rough time estimate on it, slipped it under the door and drove back home.

A few days later I forgot all about my friend and carried on with work as normal. I was taking my lunch break and who walks in but my friend's daughter. She looked tired and her eyes were red and I soon found out why. My friend had died from a sudden heart attack. I was devastated, but then her daughter told me that her mum had died the very evening I had driven down to see her. She had died at 6 p.m. and I had slipped my note under the door around 7 p.m. She asked me how I knew and told me that my note had been a source of great comfort and strength to her as she grieved for her mum.

It made her believe that somewhere, somehow her mum was close by. I'd love your thoughts, Theresa. Was my friend trying to say goodbye?

I wrote back to Caitlin to tell her that I strongly believe her friend's spirit was close to her immediately after her passing. Whenever there are bonds of love they cannot be broken by death. For, contrary to what many of us believe, death, like love, is a miracle.

The miracle of death

Death is something that many of us fear. Once again the Celtic tradition can be a spring of comfort and inspiration here because for the Celts death was not something to fear but to rejoice in. They believed, as I do, that when a person crosses over to the other side they go home to a place where there is no fear, pain or sorrow.

In Ireland there is a great understanding and respect for death and the mourning process. Those mourning the loss of a loved one are rarely left alone. Neighbours and family will rally round to offer their support and empathy. An ancient tradition known as the *caoineadh* involved women who came in and wailed for the departed and their presence helped the bereaved express their emotions of grief and loneliness freely. The tradition of the wake – where family and loved ones sit with the body on the first night of death – serves a similar function by providing a time of space, ritual and sorrow for the bereaved. It may also be of benefit to the recently departed as they adjust to their new life in spirit.

Perhaps one of the most intriguing Irish traditions surrounding death, and one that once again suggests how interwoven the world of spirit and the physical world are, is that of the *bean sidhe*. The sense that death is never far away is expressed in this figure of a spirit woman who can be heard or seen crying a few days before someone is about to die. The *bean sidhe* can appear in human form, typically as a beautiful but pale young maiden washing clothes, but it is far more common to hear her sing. In Leinster she is sometimes known as the *bean chaointe* or *keening woman*, whose cry is so piercing it can shatter glass. In Kerry, her singing is described as low and pleasant, in Tyrone it is more of a screech, and on Rathlin Island it is described as owl-like.

There are many stories of people, sometimes in peak health, who within a week of the cry of a *bean sidhe* being heard, meet a sudden and unexpected death. One famous incident occurred in Dublin, at 2.30 a.m. on 6 August 1801. It involved the death at his home of Lord Rossmore, commander-in-chief of the British forces in Ireland. The evening before, he had attended a party in Dublin Castle and to everyone there had seemed in perfect health. He stayed at the party until midnight and before he left he invited Sir Jonah and Lady Barrington to join a party he was holding at his house in Mount Kennedy, Co Wicklow. At two o'clock in the morning Sir Jonah Barrington woke and heard 'plaintive sounds' coming from outside his window from the garden below. His wife and maid heard the sounds too. At

2.30 a.m. Barrington heard a voice call 'Rossmore' three times and then there was silence. The next morning the Barringtons were told that Lord Rossmore was dead. His servant had heard strange sounds coming from his room and rushed in. Rossmore died at 2.30 a.m. Later Sir Jonah wrote: 'Lord Rossmore was dying at the moment I heard his name pronounced.' Sir Jonah found it frightening but to the Irish servants it was nothing to fear and no mystery because they knew it was the *bean sidhe* that Sir Jonah had heard.

To this day the *bean sidhe* tradition is still very much alive in Ireland as this next story sent to me by Angela illustrates.

Night call

I live in a very small part of Ireland which is mostly farmland and countryside and this happened to me about twenty years ago. I was seven months pregnant with my second child and finding it hard to sleep so I stayed up to read a book. It must have been about midnight when I heard what sounded like sobbing. It sounded so real that I went to the window to look outside. It was pitch dark and I could not see anything so I woke my husband who went outside to take a look but there was no one there. We decided it must be a cat or something so we went back to bed. Two hours later at 2 a.m. I woke again and heard the same cry. It was louder and stronger this time; so loud that I sat upright as it seemed to be right outside my window. I wasn't frightened of the sound. I just noticed it, if that makes sense. Then it suddenly stopped and there was silence. I checked my watch and it was 2.15 a.m.

The next morning I got a call from my sister-in-law who told me that my brother had died. I was in shock. I knew he had been in hospital for a routine operation but the operation had been a success and we had chatted on the phone a few days ago. He had sounded fine. Doctors had said he was fine. Apparently, he was staying up late happily watching TV with some friends when he suddenly collapsed and died.

It was only later at the funeral that I told my sister-in-law about the wailing I had heard. She went silent for a moment and told me that my brother had died at 2 a.m. I'd always thought the *bean sidhe* tradition was simply a story until then. I know different now.

When death is close the links between this life and the next are at their strongest and over the many years I've been a psychic writer and researcher I have collected countless stories of people catching glimpses of spirits and angels at this moment of transition. I've read many accounts of angels 'in waiting', typically angels or the spirits of departed loved ones coming to meet people who are dying, to bring them home. As far as I can understand it, the *bean sidhe* tradition highlights the enormous respect the Celtic tradition has for the miraculous possibilities of death. Most people are terrified of dying but when our time comes we will not be alone; our angels will be right beside us, guiding us into our new life in spirit. Seen in this light, death is no longer a painful ending but a joyous new beginning, as this next story sent to me by Logan illustrates so beautifully.

Hold my hand

I sat with my granddad the night he died. He fluctuated between consciousness and unconsciousness. It was clear that he was nearing the end, and doctors had told me it could be any day now. When he was lucid I could tell he was frightened. I was scared too as I had never seen anyone die. I felt powerless and angry too that the only thing I could do to help was hold his hand. I wanted him to know that he was not alone. On several occasions I felt him squeeze my hand really hard as if he was trying to say thank you.

Around four in the morning I woke with a start. My granddad was breathing very heavily and I knelt down beside him. As I did he opened his eyes and looked at me but he didn't look at me the way he had done for the past few months. There was no trace of medication or pain about him. He sparkled. Then he sat up and told me he was going to be OK. He looked so full of health and happiness I believed him. I felt tears of joy in my eyes. Then my granddad stopped looking at me and looked towards the window. I followed his gaze and was struck with a sense of awe and foreboding as I saw this bright shaft of light. It was so bright it almost blinded me. I saw the light come towards my granddad and completely cover him. I heard my granddad say my mother's name – my mum had passed away fifteen years ago – and then the light vanished as quickly as it had arrived. My granddad was still sitting up and then he yawned and slowly fell back onto his pillows. I say fell but it was actually as if someone was gently placing him down. He was smiling. I knew he had gone.

I've often asked myself if I imagined or dreamed what I saw, but each time I come to the same conclusion and that is that I was wide awake. I'm so glad I had the courage to hold my granddad's hand that night. What I saw has changed my life completely. My grandfather and I were very close and at the wake everyone told me how well I was coping. I wanted to tell them that I wasn't thinking about my grief, I was thinking about my grandfather and how he would have wanted me to celebrate his life rather than mourn it. I never really used to understand or feel comfortable with the tradition of the wake here in Ireland, but I understand it fully now after what I have seen. When a person dies they are in a state of transition. The angels will be there to guide them but we can also help them by doing all we can to ease their transition to the next life. The departed need our prayers for their journey but they also need to know that we are coping OK without them. They need us to hold their hand in this life and, sometimes, in death.

Logan's story shows that death does not have to be a negative experience. Death can be the beginning of a new relationship in spirit, not only with the person who has died but with the divine spark, the *anam cara*, that lives inside us all. This is because when we finally understand that death is not the end but a rebirth in spirit we begin to lose our sense of separation and fear. We begin to understand that we are eternal beings and that eternal life doesn't begin with death. It is within us already.

When we die our spirits are free to live in a place where there is no separation, time, fear or loneliness. Many of us want to know where this place is and yet again the Celtic tradition is so illuminating. For the Celts, the dead were not separate from us in some distant place because the world of spirit was not a place

57

but a different state of existence or being. The only difference between human and spirit was, for them, that spirit is invisible. You cannot normally see the dead but you can still sense them and feel their closeness to you in your heart because they are all around us and always within us.

I would like to slip in this Irish funeral prayer here. Although it was derived from a sermon written by Henry Scott Holland and first delivered in St Paul's Cathedral in London on 15 May 1910, versions of this sermon have been used at many Irish and Catholic funerals over the years.

Death is nothing at all.
It does not count.
I have only slipped away into the next room.
Everything remains as it was.
The old life that we lived so fondly together is untouched,
*   unchanged.*
Whatever we were to each other, that we are still.
Call me by the old familiar name.
Speak of me in the easy way which you always used.
Put no sorrow in your tone.
Laugh as we always laughed at the little jokes that we enjoyed
*   together.*
Play, smile, think of me, pray for me.
Let my name be ever the household word that it always was.
Let it be spoken without effort.
Life means all that it ever meant. It is the same as it ever was.
There is unbroken continuity.

Why should I be out of mind because I am out of sight?
I am but waiting for you, for an interval, somewhere very near,
  just around the corner.
All is well. Nothing is hurt; nothing is lost.
One brief moment and all will be as it was before.
How we shall laugh at the trouble of parting, when we meet
  again.

Angels everywhere

And last, but by certainly no means least, no chapter about Irish Angels would be complete without mention of Irish mystic Lorna Byrne and her autobiographical book, *Angels in My Hair*, published in 2008. The book is based in Ireland and talks about Byrne's spiritual communication with angels and spirits. The phenomenal success of the book, which has sold over half a million copies and been published in forty-seven countries, prompted *The Times* in September 2010 to ask if Byrne was responsible for the significant increase in Britain of people who believe in angels – up from 29 per cent to 46 per cent. More recent studies confirm that the numbers of those who believe in angels is steadily growing.

Of course, it could be said that many factors play a part in this spiritual growth. Disillusionment with established religion has to be one of those factors, as has the growth of the internet, where people with a belief in angels can unite in greater numbers than ever before, but Byrne's writing and passion for angels has without doubt been incredibly influential. Here we have a woman who describes herself on her website as 'an ordinary person dealing with the challenges and joys of everyday life, just like you'. She lives in rural Ireland, has raised four children and lost a husband; but from an early age she has seen and heard angels. All those who have met Byrne describe her as calm and peaceful and completely normal and she has done more to encourage other ordinary people to come forward and talk about their spiritual experiences than any other person in recent decades. She has been a missionary, for want of a better word, for the angel movement. She has helped countless people discover their Celtic souls, spirits and hearts, and although her story and her message were born in Ireland they have transcended their place of origin and become an influence and a driving force all over the world.

The next chapter of this book explores further this theme of Ireland touching the lives of those not born on Irish soil. I'm going to talk about people who have visited Ireland, or encountered someone or something strongly associated with Ireland, and experienced life-changing heavenly encounters as a result.

I think you will be intrigued and inspired by what you are about to read. I'm hoping what you find will remind and reassure once and for all that you do not need to be Irish to have a Celtic soul.

CHAPTER THREE

Divine Visitors

The lucky 'coincidences' of our lives are really miracles for which God chooses to remain anonymous. And the 'luck of the Irish' is actually the grace of God, acknowledged and appreciated. Look for the hand of God in the providential happenings in your own life.

Extract from *'Tis a Blessing to be Irish*
by Rosemary Purdy (2001)

Although it is only 189 miles wide and 302 miles long, Ireland enjoys the appeal of much, much larger countries. The country's emerald green hills, endless ocean views, vivid and colourful history and rich and varied cultural life have a great deal to do with that appeal, but this chapter won't be focusing on any of these as it is not a travel guide. Instead, it is going to focus on Ireland as a place of pilgrimage and spiritual transformation.

In chapter one I talked about my first trip to Ireland, explaining how and why it became an important turning point in my life, and as I researched this book I soon discovered that I was not alone. Numerous people told me that they had had similar unexpected moments of realisation or transformation on a trip to the Emerald Isle. In some cases spiritual growth had been the very last thing on their minds. They had simply gone on holiday or to visit friends or were on a work-related trip, but had been surprised by the inspiration and peace they discovered within and around themselves. Others told me they had travelled to Ireland hoping for spiritual nourishment or renewal, but whatever the reason for their visit, all agreed that their trip had been life-changing in some profound way and unconsciously or consciously they had all gone on a pilgrimage.

What is a pilgrimage?

Pilgrimage was a very important part of ancient Celtic spirituality. The Celts took up the practice as a way of discovering their own path to the divine and the practice is still very much alive in Ireland today.

In its purest, original sense the word pilgrimage means a sacred journey to a place of great significance to a person's beliefs and faith, but as this chapter will make clear, it is a journey that is both inward and outward in nature. A person who goes on a pilgrimage is called a pilgrim and their journey is one of inspiration and fulfilment. True pilgrimage is not necessarily about a change of destination but always about a change of heart and/or mind.

The history of pilgrimages – or travel used as a way to strengthen or renew faith – dates back to the very beginnings of civilisation. Pilgrimages are strongly associated with

Christianity, Islam and Buddhism, but you do not need to belong to a particular religion to become a pilgrim. The definition of a pilgrimage, remember, is sacred travel, and if a person feels transformed in some way or rediscovers what is really important in their lives, then whether they are religious or not they have been on a pilgrimage. Like angels, pilgrimages are for everyone, regardless of religion, race or culture, so bear in mind that in this chapter the term pilgrimage is used in the general rather than religious sense; a way of connecting or finding meaning in your life.

So how does the idea of pilgrimage relate to us today? The Celtic pilgrims were searching for a connection with the divine within and around them, and today, so many hundreds of years later, anyone with a belief or interest in angels is on exactly the same journey, whether that sacred journey be on foot or in their hearts.

Sacred journeys

It could be said that travel to any country or place is a life-changing and transformative experience. Travel teaches you so many things, not only in a cultural way but in a personal way, because when you are in a new environment and out of your comfort zone you learn new things about yourself. For instance, you gain a greater tolerance of things and people being different from what you are used to. You learn to live without things you normally rely on, you learn to cope with situations that are out of your control, like delays and weather and – this is especially the case if you travel solo – you learn to rediscover yourself, who you are and what your priorities are. Whether consciously or not, travel always serves as a spur for some kind of personal growth.

Admittedly, there are many more ways travelling can open your mind, but just because you have travelled widely does not mean you will transform into a whole new person. Some people will and some people won't, as it all depends on how open and receptive you are to your new environment, and in many cases transformation takes time. The seeds are planted and gradually priorities change and without even realising it you become a different person, more willing to step outside your comfort zone and less defined by the opinions of others. For me, the vital skill that travelling can teach us is observation. It can help you be constantly in an observant state, and when you are in this state you are fully present, and this is a form of meditation because meditation is simply the art of observing what is going on around and within you. Think about it. When you are exposed to a place that is new or different, you are out of your usual routines and your normal thought processes are not useful or relevant. As you make this leap into the unknown, for a split second your mind is baffled. You become utterly still and in this stillness you observe what is going on around you. Without mental energy wasted on endless thought processes you feel alert but peaceful and calm. You feel intensely alive in the here and now – the present moment.

It takes vast amounts of self-awareness to know that all this is going on within you. You might simply think it is down to the stimulus of travel and try to travel as much as possible to experience these feelings. But it is not in fact travel that is giving you feelings of wellbeing but the experience of your mind becoming quiet – the new location you are in is simply giving your mind a gentle nudge in the right direction.

Put simply, travel is an enlightening experience, but the real journey is one that can never be taken on foot, and that is the journey to your spirit. In the words of Joseph Campbell, 'You are that mystery which you are seeking to know.' The outward journey is simply a symbol of the inner journey; a journey in search of purpose and spirit. So, although travel is helpful and stimulating, it is not absolutely essential for your spiritual growth.

Having said that, travel can act as a medium for spiritual growth and, as you'll see in this chapter, this is especially the case when it comes to Ireland. From the numerous accounts I have read and heard, Ireland is not just any place to travel. Lives, hearts and minds can be changed forever after a visit to the Emerald Isle, and this next story, about Oscar-winning director Stephen Spielberg's recent trip to Ireland, is as good a place as any to begin.

My life transformed

Oscar-winning director Steven Spielberg described a 2009 summer vacation to Ireland as 'life-changing'. Of course, this was not Spielberg's first trip to Ireland: the D-Day scenes in *Saving Private Ryan* were filmed in Ballinesker Beach in County Wexford. This trip, however, was not work-related but for pleasure and the superstar director said he was 'transformed' by his visit, which included literally 'hanging over the edge' of the Cliffs of Moher.

The trip almost turned to disaster when Spielberg fell on the Burren and dislocated his knee. Fortunately, a local doctor was able to snap the knee back into place, enabling the director to recuperate and enjoy a glass of Guinness in O'Loughlin's pub in Ballyvaughan, County Clare. While he was there he said he was 'spellbound' by the local musicians and felt more relaxed than ever before. Later, on a trip to the Aran Islands, he rode a motorbike and ate fish and chips with the locals.

As well as enjoying listening to poetry on the jagged cliffs of the Aran Islands, and soaking up quiet village life in the Burren, Spielberg enjoyed the natural wonders of Ireland while on walking and cycling tours. The trip ended just outside Dublin and, before returning to work, Spielberg said that everyone he met had been very good to him and his mind, soul and body felt refreshed after the trip. It had been simply life-transforming.

Land of many ruins

One of the first things you may notice when you visit Ireland is that it is a country of many ruins. Scattered all over the stunning countryside are reminders of the past. On their pilgrimages the Celts would often leave lasting signs of their journey, such as crosses or small mounds of pilgrims' stones called cairns. These stones were symbols of prayers or parts of their journey completed. Ovatories and sundials can also be seen, as can bullaun stones with basins for healing water, and arcs, which are flat stones with arcs carved to form a cross. Round towers were significant during times of pilgrimage as they could be used for shelter from bad weather or attack and, as they could be seen for miles, they provided pilgrims with inspiration and perhaps even served as direction markers.

Today many of these stones and towers and other artefacts are in ruins but they are still regarded as places of sacred presence for pilgrims to gather or to remind individuals of the nearness of heaven. They are not empty or abandoned in any way, as this next story from Jonathan shows.

Took my breath away

I'm a history teacher and I've been to many historical sites, but the only one that has moved me to tears was my trip to the Rock of Cashel in southern Ireland. It took my breath away and has convinced me that the life and heart of a person leaves its imprint on a place.

When my friend suggested we go there my first reaction was, what is the big deal about a rock? How wrong I was. From the moment I saw it I knew I was going somewhere extraordinary. We travelled by car and, after passing through farmland, we turned a corner in the road and all of a sudden saw this stunning ruined abbey sitting on top of a rocky fist. The history of the place is astonishing. I'm not going to go into it here, but I'd highly recommend doing some reading on Cashel as you will be amazed.

The highlight of the tour for me was the tremendous view. While I was taking it all in I am sure I actually heard voices. I'm not being crazy here – I heard voices from the past. I heard kings speak. I heard battle cries and I heard prayers. I heard tears and I heard laughter. I did not imagine it and there was no audiotape running. This experience was real for me. All my life I have sought to make history come alive for my students but it was only there on the top of the Rock of Cashel that it really came alive for me. It was a deeply spiritual experience.

The idea Jonathan is trying to articulate here is that even in ruins the spirits of those who once lived there survive in some form. The love and passion of a person do not die when they pass away; they seep into the buildings and the landscape, giving it a sacred presence, filling it with heart.

In the Celtic tradition this sense or awareness that the dead are never far away is all-pervading, and all over Ireland there are numerous ruins, homes, fields and so on where stories circulate of dead people being seen. These stories became part of folk-lore, a tradition that acknowledges that people who have once lived in a certain place remain there in their invisible form, but, as you'll see in Emily's story below, it is not just famous ruins or castles where these stories are born.

An angel called my name

I'm convinced that the three-bedroom town house I grew up in in Limerick City is occupied by spirits. I'd use the term haunted but that has negative associations for many people and there was nothing negative about my experiences there as a child. I always felt protected and safe.

There were many incidents of doors opening and closing by themselves and I would often hear someone walking upstairs when I knew there was no one there. One of the most memorable incidents happened when I was eleven years old. I woke up in the middle of the night and heard a young woman's voice call my name. It was such a gentle, sweet voice it didn't scare me. This happened on and off for the next few months. I told my mum about it and one night she stayed with me in the room and heard it too.

I'm really writing to you though to talk about something extraordinary that happened to me last month. After Mum and Dad died I considered putting the house up for sale. Instead of comforting me, all the happy memories of living there were making me sad. One evening I was tidying up some of Mum's things and saw a woman standing in the hallway of the house. She had her face turned away from me and my first thought was that I must have left the door open and she had walked in. I grabbed my mobile and started to call the police but at that moment she turned to look at me and it was my mum. I looked her in the eyes. It was her. She was real. My mum didn't seem to notice me. She was just looking intently into the kitchen, a place where she used to spend hours talking, laughing, reading and cooking.

The incredible moment ended when my phone started to buzz with an incoming text. I looked down at it and when I looked up Mum was gone. After that I decided not to put the house up for sale. I can't bear to think of Mum living there with strangers.

Continuing the theme of ruins filled with spirits, I feel I must mention the distinctive sets of stones called dolmens which can be found across Ireland. A dolmen consists of two or more large tablets of limestone standing next to each other with a gap in between and supporting a large flat horizontal capstone on top of them. They probably date back to between 3000 and 2000 BC and are generally thought to be tombs – they are also known as portal tombs – although their original significance is still unknown. There are around 100 dolmens scattered around Ireland in various states of repair. It is hard to understand how people managed to manipulate these massive capstones into place but the fact that the stones are still standing is testament to the incredible skill and dedication of the people who erected them.

In the Celtic tradition dolmens were known as 'Leaba Dhiarmada agus Grainne', which means the bed of Diarmuid and Grainne. The legend tells of a tragic love story similar to that of King Arthur and the romance between his wife Guinevere and his right-hand man Sir Lancelot. The beautiful Grainne was promised to marry the Celtic warrior Fionn but she fell in love with Diarmuid and the two eloped together and hid all over Ireland with Fionn in hot pursuit. Often the lovers would shelter in dolmens at night. Their story ended tragically when Fionn finally caught up with them and refused to give the dying Diarmuid the drink that would save his life, leaving Diarmuid to die in his lover's arms.

The most likely explanation for the dolmens is that they were ancient burial places, but in my mind the legend speaks more eloquently about the rejuvenating power of love – even love that ends tragically, as this next story from Cecily illustrates so well.

Striking a chord

I was on a research trip to Ireland for the magazine I work for. I'd been commissioned to do a series of articles on 'Supernatural Ireland' and the trip couldn't have come at a better time as my boyfriend of eleven years had recently cut my heart in two by sleeping with my best friend. Before I left I made the decision to never trust my heart again because it had been wrong. From now on my head was going to do the talking. I felt bitter and resentful that I had wasted more than a decade on a relationship that was a lie. How I wished I had invested less time in my relationship and more in my career. I might have been an editor now instead of a freelancer.

So I began my trip with a very bitter mindset but that all changed when I started researching and visiting the dolmens in County Clare, County Carlow and County Armagh to name but a few. I researched all the stories about ghost sightings and all the legends associated with the dolmens, but the one that really spoke to me on a personal level was that of Diarmuid and Grainne. I got a bit obsessed with it. I began to see that when you fall in love you do put common sense aside. Diarmuid and Grainne could have saved themselves a whole lot of heartache if they had denied their passion, but they would also have denied themselves the reviving power of love. Longing and passion can cause pain and heartache but without them there can be no magic. I began to understand that a heart that has never loved is more tragic than a heart that has been broken. Without love and passion my spirit would have withered and the eleven years I spent with my boyfriend were not wasted years.

I'm writing to you, Theresa, because in your books you tell me that angels speak to us in deeply personal ways and I wanted to ask you if you thought that my angel spoke to me through this beautiful legend. When I started my trip I fully intended to shut my heart down but after it I understood that this is no way to live. I've met someone new and am in love again. Yes, I'm frightened that it may all end in tears but I would rather that than a life without love.

I wrote back to Cecily to thank her wholeheartedly for her unusual and fascinating perspective. I agree with her completely that a life without love is more tragic than a broken heart and we should never be afraid to open our hearts. Cecily is talking about physical love here, but I think what she says could just as well apply to spiritual love: the longing for a sense of completeness and understanding that exists within all our hearts and which is fast becoming a feature of twenty-first-century life.

From the volume of letters and emails I receive it is clear to me that a craving for the world of spirit is coming alive within very many of us. As this book goes to print it will be 2012, a year filled with doomsday predictions, but for me the real significance of 2012 – the true revolution and transformation – is the emergence of a new form of consciousness that does not have as its foundation, religious belief, rules or rituals, but a wonderful respect for the mystery, depth and uniqueness of each and every soul. And in its recognition that each soul is different and that each one of us must develop our own personal relationship with the divine, Celtic mysticism stands at the forefront of this emerging new consciousness.

Moving on from the dolmens I'd like to briefly mention another kind of Irish landmark associated with transformation and healing: sacred springs. In ancient times the land of Ireland was said to be the body of the goddess, the spiritual power of the universe. Wells were therefore regarded as sacred places where it was possible to glimpse the threshold between the unknown and the surface of the landscape. To this day people still visit sacred springs in Ireland hoping for physical and spiritual healing. They will typically walk around the well and leave gifts. For some people, like Shelley whose story is below, visiting a sacred well can awaken new possibilities.

Deep down

Six months ago I visited Saint Brigid's Well in County Kildare. It was the most surreal experience and one I feel compelled to write to you about. I'd heard that it was a healing well and although I didn't expect any miracles I thought I had nothing to lose by going there and praying for healing for my arthritis. It mostly affected my jaw; some days it was so bad I couldn't even open my mouth to eat because of the pain.

When I got there I saw that the well area is surrounded by an iron fence and I had to enter through a gate. I could see that people had left a variety of offerings and that it was clearly still a pilgrimage site. It was very moving to see these people come forward with such hope in their eyes. I got talking to the family ahead of me and found out they had come all the way from Spain to pray for their little girl who had recently been diagnosed with cancer. She was with them and her father proudly introduced her to me. She was about fifteen years old and frighteningly thin but she had a wonderful smile and it was impossible not to feel sorry for her. When we got through the gates I don't know what came over me but instead of praying for my ailments all I could think about was that girl and her family and so I prayed for them instead of myself.

I shall never know if my prayers were heard but what I do know is that after my trip to the well I have not had any jaw or joint pain to date. My life is pain free and I can't help but wonder if what happened at Saint Brigid's Well had anything to do with it. It is not just the pain that has left me; something else has vanished inside me as well and that is any fear that this life is not all there is. I thought I believed in heaven before but now I know I believe in it and this belief has completely revitalised my life. I was settling down into old age before my visit to the well but now I feel young and alive again, even though I will be seventy-five next year.

After her visit Shelley found within herself a depth and passion for life she did not know she had. You could describe her experience as one of both physical healing and spiritual awakening. Our inner angels cannot awaken when we close our minds and our hearts with feelings of fear and lack of self belief. The key to the lock is really on the inside when it comes to spiritual awakening. We have to open it from within our hearts.

Finding heaven in thin places

If you do ever get a chance to travel through Ireland I hope you find a way to experience (just as the ancient pilgrims would have done centuries ago) another major aspect of Celtic mysticism: the immediate existence of the sacred in everything, especially in the beauty of nature. Places which were said to most closely reveal the presence of the divine were called 'thin places'. In these places it was believed that the veil between this world and the next was at its thinnest and heaven could feel earth and earth could feel heaven. Thin places could be ruins, dolmens, wells, sacred buildings or natural landscapes – most especially settings connected with water, oak trees and hilltops. Places where people died and where their bodies were buried were also thin places.

It really isn't hard to find thin places in Ireland. There is so much natural beauty to feast your eyes upon. The bewitching forests, rolling emerald hills, craggy rocks and spectacular views all suggest the beauty of heaven on earth. You've already read about how just one week in Ireland transformed the life of Steven Spielberg, but here's what happened to James. He's no movie director, but he too has a fascinating story to share.

Overwhelmed

In my gap year Ireland was just one of the places I wanted to visit, along with many others. I ended up staying there for the whole year. I fell in love with the place. *Lonely Planet* describes Ireland as 'one of Europe's gems, a scenic extravaganza of lake, mountain, sea and sky that's gorgeous enough to make your jaw drop'. Add to that a fascinating history, great literature and people with hearts of gold and you'll understand why I spent a year on the Emerald Isle travelling north, south, east and west, drinking in the sights and meeting some extraordinary people.

I'm writing to you about my gap year because it really changed my life. My parents both died before I was thirteen and I was raised by my aunt and uncle. They loved and cared for me but I never really felt like I belonged anywhere. I always had this deep hurt and a longing inside me for my parents, but after a few months in Ireland the hurt and longing gave way to a sense of peace and comfort. To my knowledge my mum and dad never visited Ireland but I do know that my mum always wanted to move there before she got ill. I can understand why and I hope that through me she got her wish.

Again, I don't want this chapter to sound like a travel guide so I'm not going to discuss or recommend 'thin places' in Ireland that you may want to visit. Instead I would like you to ponder this concept of a meeting place between heaven and earth and think about your own thin places. Where and when does heaven reach out to you? However tired or disillusioned you may feel there must be moments in your life when you cannot help but gasp in wonder: a rainbow, a sparkling blue sky, radiant sunset, inspiring music or the laughter of a child. Each one of us has those special places or times when the veil between heaven and earth feels thin. Recently, I had one of these moments. My eyes felt tired as I was working on the computer. As always I was behind schedule and feeling pressured, but then a shaft of sunlight shone through the window. It only lasted a few moments but the warmth I felt on my face lit me up on the inside. I can't explain why but I just felt happier, and it is moments like these that remind me of the closeness of my guardian angel.

As above, so below

Another important theme in Celtic spirituality is the way the ancient Celts expressed their belief through symbols and art. Just as their love of the divine compelled them on pilgrimages it also inspired them to artistic expression using metal, wood, stone, paint, music and words. Celtic designs featuring distinctive interconnecting patterns that suggest that all things are divinely related can be found all over Ireland and are beautiful and detailed symbolic representations of love, belief and faith. Representing their spiritual beliefs and practices, the symbols of the ancient Celts tell the story of their lives. Even everyday objects were decorated with pictures and symbols, consecrating the ordinary in people's idea of the divine. These symbols, or should I say statements of faith, are still found on stones, monuments and cairns at ancient sites throughout Eire and the British Isles.

There are hundreds of different Celtic symbols united by the main theme of all things holy being related, but two of the most common are Celtic spirals and crosses. For those unfamiliar with their meaning, the Celtic spiral design is a symbol of eternal life. The whirls represent the continuous creation of the universe; the passage between the spirals symbolises divisions between life, death and rebirth. The interlacing of continuous lines and spirals symbolises the strong connection between the physical and spiritual worlds and the never-ending characteristic of spirals and loops symbolises once again eternal life. The Celtic cross is one of the most cherished and well-known Celtic symbols in Ireland and represents the ancient but forever current premise, 'As above, so below.' It is the ring at their centre that makes Celtic crosses unique. In Celtic spirituality the circle/wheel represents the sacred and eternal connection of all things in heaven and earth.

There are over 100 Celtic High Crosses in Ireland and they range in height from 9 to 15 ft and each part of the cross is a sacred symbol once again representing divine interconnection with earth. Some crosses were erected just outside churches and monasteries, others at sites that may have marked boundaries or crossroads, but over the years many of these crosses have become damaged by exposure to the elements so they have been moved indoors. Inside or out, the crosses that remain are still powerful and imposing symbols of faith.

One of the most well-known High Crosses is called Muiredach's High Cross. Dating back to the tenth or possibly ninth century, and located at the ruined monastic site of Monasterboice, County Louth, Muiredach's Cross has been described as the most beautiful specimen of Celtic stonework in existence and it certainly inspired Jane, as her story below shows.

Hand-crafted

I suffered from artist's block for several months last year. I tried to do all I could to get my passion and inspiration back but nothing helped. I'm a freelance artist and with deadlines stacking up you can imagine how scared I was. This could have finished me. I was ready to turn to drink when my salvation came in the most unlikely form. A friend of mine had recently gone on a vacation to Ireland and they brought me back a hand-crafted miniature of the Muiredach Cross.

I'm not joking: the very moment I held this cross and studied its intricate designs something lit up inside me again. I actually wanted to get back to work. Ideas came flooding back and I have never felt so creative. I'm writing to you to ask if you think the cross was behind this surge of creativity, or if it was simply coincidence.

I wrote back to Jane to tell her that coincidences are the language angels speak and that since she was an artist her guardian angel had spoken to her through the medium of art because it had personal significance to her.

Something similar happened to Tracy on a trip to Ireland when she first saw the famous Book of Kells, a stunningly beautiful and expressive work of art produced in the ninth century by monks in the monastery on Iona, a small island off the Scottish coast, and sent to Dublin in 1653. It is now on display at Trinity College in Dublin and consists of a Latin text of the four Gospels, lavishly illustrated by intricate and beautiful Celtic designs. Tracy's story speaks for itself.

Painstaking

It was the last day of my trip to Ireland and I wasn't looking forward to going back home at all. I was also going back to my teaching job after missing out on a promotion to deputy head. I guess you could say I was feeling like a failure and not sure where I was going in my career or even if teaching was for me anymore. I wasn't enjoying it like I used to. I felt restless, like there had to be something with more meaning for me to do out there.

My feelings of dissatisfaction changed though when I went to see the Book of Kells. It was a personal high point. It was awe-inspiring to think about the painstaking craftsmanship and passion that it must have taken to produce this work of art; the generations of work that it took to produce this book. If I could find within myself just a fraction of that passion for my work I would not feel such dissatisfaction and restlessness within me. I mean, what greater calling could there be than inspiring young pupils to succeed in life?

Other tangible expressions of Celtic awareness of God's presence in everyone and everything can be found in Celtic literature, dance and music. This book isn't the place to review Irish poets, authors and artists, but for a modern-day celebration of Celtic music and passion you need look no further than the hugely well received *Riverdance*. The dance troupe was a revelation in every sense of the word when it first came to public attention as a filler show between votes on the Eurovision Song Contest.

I just love this story, reported in the *Irish News* in May 2009. I think you will too.

Tapping toes

Japanese man Taka Hayashi was so enthralled by the *Riverdance* show he saw on a night out that he decided to give up his job, empty his bank account and travel to Ireland to chase his dream of learning Irish dance.

The 28-year-old IT consultant had never danced in his life but remained convinced that he could audition successfully for the world-famous Irish dance troupe. His father, a Tokyo taxi driver, told his son that his dream was 'mad', but Taka was determined to succeed. He told his father that the show had changed his life and is quoted as saying: 'I realised at that moment what I wanted from my life – to be a Riverdancer.' So, without any hesitation or doubt, Taka resigned from his job, an almost unheard-of thing to do in Japan, withdrew his life savings and flew to Ireland in November 2001.

Taka travelled to Cork in search of someone who could teach him the history of Irish dance. The teacher didn't help him very much and the locals could not understand him; children called him 'Chinese' and threw stones at him. He applied for dozens of dance schools but they all rejected him, saying he was too old to be considered. Unable to find a teacher he gave up looking and started teaching himself by practising to *Riverdance* videos for up to eight hours a day.

Taka's big break eventually came when he was spotted at a *Riverdance* workshop by former Riverdancer Ronan McCormack. Ronan was astonished at how much Taka had learned just by watching videos and decided to teach him. Four months later, Taka won Intermediate Grade in his second Feis and in 2003 was selected to be a dancer in a performance of *Riverdance* at the opening of the Special Olympics in Croke Park. In 2004 he competed in the World Championships and in 2005 his dreams came true when he auditioned successfully for *Riverdance*. Ironically, his first official tour took place in the Far East, including Japan and his hometown of Tokyo, where his proud father attended the show.

Today, Taka runs a flourishing Irish dance academy in Tokyo with his wife Etsuko, also a dancer. They are both passionate about Irish dance and say that the Irish bodhran and Irish flute have similarities with the Japanese taiko and shakuhachi. It is the wonderful music and the synchronicity of the tapping feet that inspires them most. They, like thousands of others, believe that Irish dance is a bridge – a uniting force – for all cultures.

Taka's story is a charming reminder of the power of passion to transform lives. Moving on now from art I want to discuss another inspiring thing you are bound to notice if you travel to Ireland and that is the strong sense of community.

The ancient Celts placed a big focus on relationships, not just with angels and the spirits but with one another. This could perhaps explain why from the sixth century to the twelfth century, communities tended to flourish around monasteries. People who did not want to become monks or nuns but still wanted to live a life of faith and devotion found comfort and inspiration from being able to live and worship with their spiritual leaders. One of the most famous monastic communities is Glendalough, situated in Glendalough, County Wicklow. Glendalough is set in the valley of two lakes and is a major tourist attraction today. The gateway into Glendalough monastic site is the only one of its kind left standing in Ireland. The arch is held together by pressure. No cement was used! Legend has it that the bricks will fall down three days before the end of the world.

Kevin sent me this intriguing story about his visit to Glendalough.

All about Kevin

I visited Glendalough back in 2003 and it had the most incredible impact on my life. There was just something about the place that changed me forever, made me rethink everything. Perhaps it was the natural beauty or the sense of community among the locals or perhaps it was the fact that it is so strongly associated with my namesake – St Kevin! I don't know what it was but when I came back home I really took a long hard look at my life. I didn't like what I saw anymore.

I started by downsizing. I found out all the things that really matter to me. I understood that no matter how much money I earned, no matter how much I had or saved it would not make me feel secure unless I felt secure inside. I have about half of what I had eight years ago but it does not matter to me because I remind myself that I have enough for what I want and need. I also do regular volunteer work and make sure that what I work on is of benefit not just to me but to other people or the environment. I have never been happier and would never want to go back to life as it was for me. I was successful and wealthy then but I was not happy or at peace.

I'm not suggesting here that you downsize, I just wanted to include Kevin's story to illustrate the theme of generosity and community spirit which seems to burn brightly in Ireland. When visiting Ireland people from all different backgrounds, ages, cultures, races and religions seem to find ways to unite around their enjoyment of the Irish experience.

As you can see from her story below, Emma led a troubled life before she moved to Ireland and discovered who she really was.

Wild child

I left school because I was a wild child and didn't want to abide by the rules. In fact I hated school. I longed to get a sign from the other world but got scared and drugs took over. Three years ago I moved to Ireland to get away from the drugs and it was the best thing I have ever done as I'm clean now. If I hadn't moved to Ireland and got healthy I probably wouldn't have my beautiful daughter. Ireland and my daughter keep me clean and from going back to that sordid life of drugs. I think she has been sent by an angel to rescue me and her dad.

Emma also believes that since moving to Ireland she has started to get signs from the other side.

The pictures I'm sending you were taken last Christmas when we had the bad snow. I was taking photos of the snow on our street. When I looked at two photos I noticed the same shaft of light in the shape of a figure in both of them. At the time my daughter was still in the neo-natal ward with a few problems and had spent Christmas in there, which was upsetting. I just wanted her home and cried a lot, which was natural, but when I looked at those photos I got an overwhelming thought that everything would be fine with my baby and it was. I still get that wonderful feeling when I look at the photos now. I just know it was my angel trying to reassure me.

I couldn't think of a better place than here to put this next story sent to me by Sonia.

Heaven on earth

Although I enjoy reading your angel books – some of them bring tears to my eyes – one thing you haven't mentioned in your books and I would like to mention is how places can bring you closer to heaven. For me the one place where I feel touched by heaven is Ireland. It's not just the splendour of the Emerald Isle, it is the charm of the people. My husband is a committed atheist and really antisocial but even he goes all misty-eyed and gets really chatty when we visit and – although he would never admit it – I have a sneaky suspicion that each time we visit Connemara he questions his lack of faith.

There's no doubt that, alongside the stunning scenery, a not inconsiderable part of the Irish experience is the hospitality of the people there and, as this next story from Yvonne shows, it can heal many a tired, broken and disillusioned heart.

Irish inspiration

When I retired from my job in local government after thirty years' service I was at a bit of a loss. My kids had flown the nest and my husband was quite happy to do as little as possible apart from studying his family tree, so I was at a loss what to do with myself. I tried to do some volunteer work but soon realised that my contribution wasn't really valued as there were too many of us volunteers. I joined a book club and took up ballroom dancing but none of it really satisfied me and within a year of retiring I found myself getting tearful and emotional on a regular basis. I went to my doctor who put me on antidepressants and things got worse from there. I lost all sense of purpose and meaning.

Help came from the most unexpected source and that source was my husband. Seeing what distress I was in he told me that he wanted us both to go and live in Ireland. He was one-eighth Irish and was convinced that we would enjoy life more there. I wasn't convinced but I would have agreed to go anywhere, I felt so low and disillusioned.

Six months later we had sold our house in London and moved to a lovely cottage in Ireland. It was the best decision I have ever made for my mind, body and spirit. Almost immediately I noticed that retired people down here don't retire. They sing, they laugh, they gossip and they get busy living. They don't sit around worrying and fretting about things or moaning about their health. I don't know what their secret is but I do know that they laugh more. The last three years have been the happiest and most active of my life. Barely a day goes by when I don't meet someone with stories to tell and kindness to share. I don't have a drop of Irish blood in me but I have a strange sense of familiarity with everyone down here. The Emerald Isle has healed my spirit, Theresa, in much the same way as the guardian angel stories you write about in your lovely books.

Yvonne's story reminds me of that William Butler quote, 'There are no strangers here, only friends you haven't met yet.' Yvonne found a sense of belonging in Ireland but it wasn't the place that uplifted her so much as the attitude of the people there.

Irish people are typically generous and warm-hearted to whoever crosses their path. They love their land and each other but also extend a hand of friendship to anyone they encounter. What may be thought of as two distinct entities, people and land, merge together into a beautiful vision of hospitality and welcome, representing the true essence of Ireland and ensuring that the many who visit Ireland experience not just wonderful landscapes but warm handshakes along the way. I can't help but think how much richer all our lives would be if we could all reach out to each other in the same way.

Celtic spirituality today

Whether you are Irish or not I hope what you have read so far will have made it clear that Celtic spirituality has much of value to offer today. The ancient Celts were a deeply spiritual people, but since I define spirituality as how each one of us connects personally to the divine, I feel there is much we can take from Celtic spirituality and much we can make our own.

As we've seen, one way to gain an understanding of Celtic spirituality and make it come alive is to journey to Ireland, but if it isn't possible to do this it is possible to experience it from within, through the Celtic soul conviction that heaven can be found within us and in all things.

One of my favourite angel blessings pretty much sums this up:

Angels around us, angels beside us, angels within us.
Angels are watching over you when times are good or stressed.
Their wings wrap gently around you,
Whispering you are loved and blessed.

You may find it hard to imagine Celtic spirituality outside of Ireland, but remember that a pilgrimage can take place physically and spiritually. In other words, you can incorporate Celtic spiritual principles into your life right now in your own home area. Visiting 'thin places' does not have to involve travelling around Ireland but can be any place where you feel especially close to heaven. Perhaps it is a cemetery where a loved one is buried or a beautiful place in nature where you feel relaxed and calm. Perhaps it is somewhere where you have special memories of your children or loved ones or perhaps it is whenever you see a rainbow or hear birdsong. Thin places can be anywhere you want at any time.

The Celts also celebrated kinship with their fellow human beings and this is something you can do at any time with your loved ones, family, friends, colleagues or even people you don't know very well. We may look or sound different and have different stories to tell but we all have the same beating hearts. And we can also use our unique gifts to express feelings of love, passion and joy for others to be inspired or uplifted by. We may not reach the heights of artistic expression seen in the Book of Kells or *Riverdance*, but it is not the end product, rather the intention that speaks to our hearts and transforms lives.

Sure, travelling to Ireland can help connect you deeply to Irish spirituality and make the lessons learned more obvious, but remember, a pilgrimage to discover your Celtic soul is, above all, an inner journey. And whether the journey is actual or interior, what matters most is not where you are heading but what is going on in your heart – the journey of faith you are making. If you'd like to explore further this concept of pilgrimage within and the modern relevance of Celtic spirituality, may I take this opportunity to recommend a heart-opening book written in 1998 by Sister John Miriam Jones entitled *With an Eagle's Eye: A Seven-Day Sojourn in Celtic Spirituality*. It does have a Christian bias but transcends religion with its emphasis on Celtic prayers and blessings as a source of inspiration, reflection and transformation.

Land of saints and scholars

And there can be no better companions on your personal journey of faith than the invisible angels and spirits that are always walking beside you. As we've seen, in the Celtic world-view the invisible world of spirit was a natural part of creation. Being invisible did not make it any the less real but more so because it was not limited by the restrictions of space and time. Spiritual beings were soul companions and throughout their lives believers acknowledged the presence of unseen witnesses both within and around them and sought their guidance and protection.

People even greeted each other with an acknowledgement that a person's angel was close by. Angels could be encountered anywhere at any time, and there were 'thin places' where encounters were more likely, but in addition to angels and the spirits of departed loved ones, there was also an acknowledgement of the unseen presence of the saints.

Over the centuries Ireland has become known as the Land of Saints and Scholars. If you have ever travelled to Ireland and you didn't hear mention of Irish saints while you were there I'd be very surprised. There are literally hundreds of Irish saints and many Irish people live their lives with a deep awareness and veneration for them. The word 'saint' is strongly associated with Christianity and because angels are truly non-denominational and spiritual rather than religious beings I did think long and hard about even mentioning the saints in this book. However, I came to the conclusion that the book just would not be complete without some talk of Irish saints and their angels.

Visions of angels have figured in the lives of practically all the Irish saints, but please don't think you have to be religious or that you need to call upon the saints for divine guidance. As I always stress, anyone can get in touch with angels and you do not need rituals, saints or belief systems to do so. Angels, like love, are for everyone. I'm simply hoping that reading about some well-known glimpses of heaven on earth will inspire you to believe that you too can live in the presence of mystery and awe.

There are enough miraculous stories about Irish saints to fill books. Indeed, many such books have been written and

I encourage you to search them out as they are awesome to discover and there isn't room in this book to do them justice. The proliferation of Irish saints is all the more incredible when you consider that only a few of them have actually been canonised. The majority belong to the period before 800 AD, but the message they brought to the world and the legacy they leave behind is so much bigger than any one era or religion. These people transcended the accident of place and time, not only by inspiring people of their own era but continuing to inspire us down the centuries. Even today we can look at their lives and their examples and use them as a source of inspiration for our own spiritual paths. I also think their stories demonstrate that what is so often considered divine inspiration is often nothing more complicated than the angel within, or the selfless desire to serve or inspire others, acting without fear or self-regard. Whatever race, religion, colour or creed you are, I hope whatever you decide to read or learn about Irish saints will inspire you to believe that you too can be more deeply connected to heaven than you ever thought you could be.

The first name that immediately springs to mind for many of us when discussing Irish saints has to be that of Saint Patrick. Although he is the best-known Irish saint I must stress that Patrick wasn't in fact Irish; he was actually born around 390 AD in Roman Britain. As a teenager he was kidnapped and carried off to Ireland, where he was enslaved as a shepherd for six years. Eventually he managed to escape but some time later he would return and play a pivotal part in making Ireland the only land to introduce Christianity without bloodshed.

Patrick was familiar with Celtic spirituality from his enslavement in Ireland and he looked for similarities between belief systems rather than differences. He travelled widely in Ireland, opening monasteries and schools. Traditionally, Patrick's mission began in 432 AD, and according to tradition he is buried in Downpatrick, not far from the site of what is believed to be his first church at Saul, County Down. Saint Patrick's Day is celebrated on the anniversary of his death on 17 March. He is invoked by 83 million Irish people all over the world with the following: *Bail Phadraigh ar a ndeanfaimid* – Patrick's bless in all we do.

Without doubt Saint Patrick is of great importance, not just because of what he did in Ireland and the wonderful stories about him, but because of what he symbolises. To this day, all around the world Saint Patrick's Day is a day of celebration and joy to help those with Irish blood in their veins remember and rediscover their spiritual roots, but it is vitally important to remember that even though he stands for everything Irish Saint Patrick himself was NOT Irish, proving what I have been saying all along in this book: you do not have to be Irish to have a Celtic soul. So, to this day Saint Patrick's Day is also a powerful reminder to all those without Irish blood in their veins of the importance of connecting with the deep spirituality that burns within them.

Without doubt, over the years the Irish have played a vital role in keeping the flame of spirituality alive. Thomas Cahill, in his book *How the Irish Saved Civilisation*, wrote about the monks who protected this spiritual light and kept it burning during the

Dark Ages in Europe when so much spirituality died. It is this indomitable spiritual flame which makes so many people feel affectionate towards the Irish, and more than any other Irish saint it is Saint Patrick who gave this spirituality direction and meaning by fusing together Celtic spirituality and Christianity. Without his work the spiritual evolution of the world would be very different, but he isn't the only well-known saint associated with Ireland – Saint Brigid, Saint Valentine and Saint Columba are but a few of the others.

As symbols of the divine, and inspired by their piety, devotion, compassion and deep spirituality, many people still pray to Irish saints today. The practice is often challenged by those who believe that God should be the only recipient of our prayers, but saints, just like angels, are symbols or expressions of the divine within and around us and there is nothing wrong with praying to either. Remember, there is no right or wrong way to talk to heaven. If praying to saints or angels helps you feel closer to heaven then it is the right approach for you. As this next story from Sue shows, praying to a favourite saint can be a source of comfort and healing.

Lighting a candle

I really needed a holiday. I hadn't had one for three years. As well as being a single mum looking after my three children aged ten, fourteen and fifteen and working full-time, I had my 80-year-old mother to worry about. She lived alone and needed a lot of help running errands, especially since her arthritis had got worse. A home help did call round to check up on her once or twice a day and neighbours were attentive, but I still thought I should be close at hand. My mother, of course, was having none of it and when she found out that a friend was offering to let us stay in a villa in Spain for two weeks free of charge she told me in no uncertain terms to go.

The first week or so of the holiday was incredible. The kids soaked up the sun and I soaked up the sheer pleasure of having nothing to do and nowhere to go. I called my mum twice a day to check that she was all right but on the day before we were due to fly back she didn't answer the phone. I panicked and phoned again and again but there was still no reply. I called her home help and felt even more panicked when she told me that earlier that day my mum had been coming home from the shops and had had a 'flat drop' – in other words she had fallen flat on her face. The home help told me that Mum was a bit bruised but being well taken care of in hospital. When I did finally manage to speak to my mum she told me she was in a lot of pain and was finding it hard to rest. I told her we'd be back the following day.

The last day of our holiday was hard to enjoy as my thoughts kept returning to my mum. I was frantic with worry. At around 4 p.m., after a day out in the countryside, we found ourselves passing a chapel built in the gothic and renaissance styles. Normally I would have been excited to stop and look inside as I love history and architecture but this time I didn't want to go inside. My children, however, were keen to explore so I told them they could look around while I waited in the car.

Fifteen minutes later my children came back to the car with cheeky smiles on their faces. I asked them if they had found it interesting and they nodded enthusiastically. My 10-year-old told me that they had all lit candles for Grandma and asked Saint Patrick (his favourite saint) and the angels in heaven to help and heal her. This touched me deeply – and calmed me down too.

The next day we arrived back home and I immediately went to visit my mother. When I saw her I noticed the bruise on her face but I was amazed to see that she was sitting up and reading. Her voice was also animated and lively. 'I don't believe it,' she said. 'Yesterday at teatime I was in so much pain I couldn't even open my eyes and now look at me. I've been up today as well and went for a walk without any pain. I haven't been able to do that all year. Isn't it amazing?'

In a state of shock I told my mum how her grandchildren had prayed to Saint Patrick and lit candles at the exact time yesterday that she felt so much better. We both shed a few tears, convinced that heaven was hovering over us.

It soon becomes apparent when you read stories like these that the message of love and healing brought into the world by Irish saints is very much alive today and if you ever get the opportunity to travel to the village of Knock in County Mayo you may be able to experience first-hand this sense of living divinity. If you have never heard the incredible stories of angel visions and miracles surrounding the church at the village of Knock you may want to check them out. There isn't time to detail them here but today Knock Shrine is an international place of pilgrimage and prayer where over 1.5 million pilgrims come every year. It is also strongly associated with the miracle of healing, as this next story about Marion Carroll, reported in local press at the time, illustrates.

Instantly cured

Marion Carroll, the eldest daughter of a well-known Athlone family, the McCormacks, was instantly cured of multiple sclerosis when she visited Knock Shrine in September 1989.

Before her visit to Knock, Marion was hovering close to death; her bodily movements had slowed down and she was totally paralysed and wheelchair-bound at her home in Carton Drive. Despite her infirmity Marion's faith and her prayers to God and the Blessed Virgin never wavered. From a child she had always been devoted to her religion and spent a lot of her spare time in church and saying the Rosary. Despite her MS she never blamed God and always thanked heaven for the love of her family and children and felt that there were many people out there who did not have the happiness she had.

It was on a Sunday in September 1989 that everything changed forever for Marion and her family. After a bout of kidney infections she felt that her end might be close and a group of friends who worked at St Vincent's Hospital in Athlone agreed to help the wheelchair- and bed-bound Marion visit the shrine. According to Marion she only agreed to go to pray for her family and to give them a few hours' break. She never prayed for herself to be cured as she had always trusted God to make the decision about whether she lived or died.

Marion was strapped to and carried on a stretcher to the statue of Our Lady of Knock and placed right in front of the main altar. Bishop O'Reilly gave her the anointing of the sick sacrament and mistakenly called her Mary. For reasons she did not understand Marion remembers feeling irritated that the Bishop got her name wrong. She then said that she got an intense pain in her heels but as soon as the pain there left, all the pain in the rest of her body disappeared. She is quoted as saying that she got a 'beautiful feeling' inside her. 'It was like a whispering breeze' that told her if the straps were removed from her stretcher she would be able to get up and walk.

Then Marion surprised everyone, including herself, by asking for the straps to be taken off. She was so restless that one of her friends decided to do as she said. As soon as the straps were removed Marion swung her legs around and stood up. Later she said that it felt like she had never had MS.

On the journey home Marion sat and drank tea and when she came close to her Carton Drive home, her husband Jimmy came out of the front door with the wheelchair. To surprise him Marion put her surgical collar back on, even though she did not need it, and you can only imagine how shocked Jimmy was when he saw his wife walk down from the steps of the ambulance.

I have no doubt many would argue that this account simply couldn't happen as MS can't be cured by faith alone, but this is not what Marion experienced and who are we to disagree with her? For my part I have seen many examples of unexplained healings and dramatic recoveries that can only be explained by a higher power, so I am inclined to believe her as I believe all the people who write to me with stories of heaven transforming their lives. For Marion, Knock Shrine was the trigger, but from the stories I have received over the last twenty-five years it is clear to me that you do not necessarily have to travel to a shrine to experience healing: angels can heal and change lives in any place. Having said that, if you ever get the chance, Knock Shrine is well worth a visit as it can offer many opportunities for stillness and peace in our souls – all so necessary in our busy and sometimes hectic world.

Do miracles still occur at Knock? This beautiful account may seem like a coincidence – but it holds very special significance for Mandy and her daughter Carrie.

Tears in my heart

After my husband and son died in a car crash five years ago I was in pieces. After six months of grieving my sister decided to book me and my daughter a holiday to Ireland; she thought it would help heal our broken hearts as it was a place I had always wanted to visit.

On the second day of our trip we went to Knock. While queuing to see the shrine I said to my daughter how brilliant it would be if we got a sign from Dad and her brother that they were together in heaven, taking care of each other. About two minutes later I looked at my daughter and a butterfly was sitting on her elbow. It looked like it was stuck in her cardigan. I was just about to gently brush it away when another butterfly appeared and landed right next to it. I was mesmerised. My daughter was lost in thought and hadn't noticed so I gently whispered to her not to move and to look down at her arm. The butterflies just sat there for about a minute as we both looked at them with tears in our eyes. Then my daughter very gently helped them fly away. They didn't fly away immediately, though – they stayed a while circling around our heads before flying away. It was the most precious and healing moment for both of us. I truly believe my husband and son came back to comfort us and it was particularly poignant that my daughter had to help them fly away; I felt like they were saying we should let go of our grief and move forward with our lives.

I wrote back to Carrie and Mandy to tell them that in Irish folklore butterflies are symbols of the soul. According to one Gaelic tradition loved ones in spirit may sometimes make themselves visible in butterfly form hovering close by their coffins, graves, or by those who are mourning them. This was a sign of eternal happiness for the soul.

Time to move away from stories about Irish saints now, but before I do I'd like to remind you once again that just as you don't need to be Irish to see angels, you don't need to be a saint, guru, medium or psychic to be inspired by heaven either. Inspiration, like angels, is for everyone. Think about it. Often the primary motivation of saints, like Saint Patrick, was to simply help, lead, or inspire others to believe in the invisible world of goodness and love. They were not perfect in every way. They were human beings, just like you and me. The only difference being that their loving intention was so powerful that it allowed them to break free from limitations, fly high and overcome seemingly insurmountable obstacles, and by so doing fill others with a lasting and profound sense of awe and wonder. Seen in this light, all of us are capable of rising above the ordinary and bringing a glimpse of heaven to earth if we simply allow ourselves to express without interference the loving intentions, or as I call it the Celtic soul, that we already have inside us.

Only the human part of us knows limitation; the angels inside and around us who are simply waiting for us to see, hear and feel them, know none.

Enchanted and inspired

It is my sincere hope that what you have read so far will have shown you that despite its often turbulent history and the recent economic crisis Ireland remains a deeply spiritual place, a place where the veil between this life and the next is often very thin. I strongly urge you to pay it a visit one day to nourish your soul, but if that isn't possible the remaining chapters in this book will show you that it is always possible to visit it in your heart.

Sure, 'tis a blessing to be Irish', but as you'll now see in the pages that follow, it is also a blessing to be born in any country, anywhere in the world, and whatever your nationality 'tis a blessing to be alive in spirit'. So prepare to be enchanted and inspired by the international stories that follow, and while you read observe how – even though the people who submitted them have no physical connection with Ireland – the ancient themes of Celtic spirituality we've been talking about reappear over and over again. Notice how these eternal themes prove their divine origin by reinventing themselves for the modern world and speaking to us through the voices of ordinary people with extraordinary experiences to share.

CHAPTER FOUR

Celtic Souls

Always remember to forget the troubles that passed away. But
never forget to remember the blessings that come each day.

Irish blessing

In Honesty
Above and beyond, love is in
The faith and hope we believe, in our hearts
And hope is all we have.
So give all you can of love, live it
Romantic and spiritual –
Love is the truth
Make love count . . .

Paul Holland *(Hearts Desires,* Forward Press, 2000*)*

Based on reports throughout their history it does seem that
Irish people are highly receptive to the spirit world and angelic
beings, but that doesn't mean that you have to be Irish or need
to visit Ireland to see angels. As I've tried to make as clear as I

can in this book so far, although Ireland can act as a catalyst, with an open mind and an open heart anyone can reawaken the inner angel or Celtic soul within them and have the special connection with angels that is their birthright. That's why all the stories that follow on from here are submitted by people who have no physical connection to Ireland. What they do have in common, though, is a deep and powerful belief in miracles.

Whether we are Irish or not, there is still an angel – a Celtic soul – in each one of us that has always believed in magic, and when we rediscover this angel we realise there is great hope. It does not matter who we are or where we were born; all that matters is what we feel and believe in. So, sit back and let what you read now remind you of something you once instinctively knew but have forgotten: that in the eyes of our angels we all have Celtic souls and hearts that yearn for healing, hope, protection, guidance and love in an often complicated and turbulent world.

I'm going to begin with a story that came to my attention through newspapers and the internet in December 2007.

An angel saved me

Nineteen-year-old Joshua Kosch was hit by a freight train in downtown Fayetteville in North Carolina in November 2007; he was wearing fancy dress at the time and was walking to an annual town festival. 'I basically dressed up in the attire appropriate for the Dickens Festival,' says Joshua, 'a Victorian-times style, and was looking forward to taking part.'

Joshua had to cross two sets of railroad tracks to get to the festival and he stood on one set of railroad tracks while waiting for a south-bound train to pass on the adjoining tracks. Unfortunately, he didn't hear the northbound train approaching behind him. The conductor did see Joshua and managed to slow the train down to 20 m.p.h. but not in time to avoid hitting him. During the accident Joshua believes he saw an angel. He said, 'He [the angel] told me it wasn't my time and I couldn't get up. And that's because he held me down.'

Joshua spent many weeks in hospital after the accident recovering from broken ribs, punctured lungs, broken vertebrae and a broken arm. He also had his right leg amputated above the knee. His mother, Barbara, says that seeing her son survive was a miracle. She said: 'It makes me stronger in my faith, knowing that God was there, right there, when it happened.'

Fast-forwarding to April 2010 and travelling over to the UK, here's another 'angel saved my life' story that captured the imagination of the newspapers at the time.

The tattoo

Eighteen-year-old Luke Fisher broke his neck in a terrible car crash. He nearly died but believes his life was saved by the guardian angel tattoo he had had done a few days before. Two days before Luke's car crashed head-on into a tree, flattening the front of his car and shattering his neck in three places, Luke had the image of a guardian angel tattooed onto his torso. Doctors thought Luke was lucky not to have died and feared he would never walk again. But Luke, whose tattoo also had the words 'Only the strong survive', defied the odds and, despite his injuries, left the hospital in a neck brace four days later.

The magnificent tattoo, which took sixteen hours to complete, was created by Gods of Ink in Barbourne, Worcestershire. It begins on Luke's right hip and goes around his body with one of the angel wings covering his chest and the other going across his back as if hugging him. Luke, who intends to join the army once he has made a full recovery, believes it definitely helped save his life. He hopes it will continue to watch over him.

Nick Fletcher, who completed the tattoo, was shocked when he heard about Luke's accident. He also believes the tattoo was a lucky charm as the accident would have killed most men.

These are just two isolated examples of 'angel saved my life' stories that have hit the headlines in recent years.

Lil's story didn't hit the newspapers in quite the same way, but this does not make it any the less remarkable.

It's a miracle

Hi, I am in the middle of reading your book *An Angel Changed My Life*. I wasn't looking to buy your book but I was drawn to it. I believed in ghosts but you've changed my view of them – now I real-ise they are actually angels and I have had a lot of encounters with them. The first happened when my 8-year-old daughter was about eight months old and sleeping in her own room. I was asleep in my bedroom when something violently shook me awake and urged me to go and check on my daughter. When I got to her room she was choking on vomit. I thank the angels for watching over us that night and saving my daughter's life.

Secondly, a few years ago my cousin had an accident. She was pronounced dead at the scene but was revived and taken to hospital. Tests were done and there was too much brain damage for her to lead any type of life so family and friends gathered around her to say their final goodbyes, but twenty minutes before the life support machines were switched off she woke up with no brain damage and was released from hospital three days later. It's a miracle that I believe only angels could have made happen.

Natasha sent me this extraordinary story.

Look both ways

I was walking to pick up my children from school and I was approaching a main road which I had to cross as usual. I looked both ways and saw that there was not a car in sight.

I was about to cross the road when I suddenly felt as though someone was behind me and pulling me backwards – with such force that I almost lost my footing. I was a little stunned and lost for words as when I looked around no one was there. I tried again to walk across the road but the force pulled me back again. It was as if someone had a hold of my arm and was pulling me backwards.

Just then I heard a loud screeching sound. I looked up and saw a young drunk driver lurching at ridiculous speeds down the road. He was driving so fast and seemed to come out of nowhere – meaning the road was completely clear one second and the next this madman was screaming down the road so fast.

I realised that it was my guardian angels and guides who were pulling me out of the road. If I had crossed the road at that point I would have been hit by the mad driver and would have been killed. I felt shaken up but thanked my angels and guides for their help and their warning.

I receive many miraculous rescue stories and in each case there is always that firm conviction that heaven lent a helping hand. When reading stories like this even the most sceptical among us may be forced to at least consider the possibility that something invisible was watching over the people involved. Many of them like to call this invisible presence their guardian angel. Indeed you may have noticed the term guardian angel cropping up rather a lot in stories like these, but what exactly do people mean when they talk about their guardian angels?

Guardian angels are spiritual beings, direct expressions of the loving thoughts of heaven sent to watch over us and help us. They are pure love and bring to us only what will help us, guide us, protect us and encourage us to aspire to the very best qualities of our soul. They can bring us light during times of darkness and if we make, or have made, choices that do not bring us closer to the light, they will show us how to let go of those choices and make more positive ones. Think of your guardian angel as your best and highest friend and supporter who can help you find solutions to challenges that you face, and help you understand that if you are willing to open your mind and heart, anything is possible. In other words, think of your guardian angel as your soul companion, your inner angel – or, to reference the previous chapters, your *anam cara*.

Your guardian angel's purpose is to help, guide or save you whenever and however possible. Sometimes heavenly salvation comes in dramatic, sensational ways, as illustrated by the stories and narratives above, but far more common and just as wonderful is when salvation comes in more subtle ways, such as inspiring us with a thought that prompts us to take positive action, or sending us a hunch or gut feeling that guides us to safety or averts potential disaster. In fact, there are many instances which are often put down to luck, coincidence or even a miracle, but which have the touch of a hand of light behind them.

Your guardian angel is also the voice inside your head urging you to follow your inner guidance and believe what your heart is telling you, no matter how crazy it may seem at the time. You have free will and your guardian angel will always walk beside you, but if you take a moment to reflect and listen there will be a voice deep inside you that wants you to choose words, thoughts, feelings and actions that bring you happiness and peace, not fear and sorrow. Your angel will be quietly and steadily sending you the voices of joy and peace in the hope you will choose what best represents these things to you.

At this point, I can almost hear you wondering to yourself why our guardian angels don't always rescue us when we are in trouble or danger; whenever I do talks about angels in bookshops or on the radio this question always comes up. My answer is always the same as I try to explain that we have the heaven-sent gift of free will and, sometimes, for reasons we may not understand in this life, our angels must stand back, giving love and support only, so we can work things out for ourselves. These are the times when we feel most alone and afraid, the darkness before the dawn, but if we can work through the darkness and discover the angel within, life will never be the same again. Whenever I read inspirational stories about someone discovering unexpected inner strength, their fighting spirit, or beating the odds, I always smile because I know the angels are at work again, even if we don't give them their name. Many people discover their guardian angel in this way and the feeling of joy and strength they gain from discovering that they are stronger and more powerful than they believed themselves to be brings a real sense of magic and possibility into their lives.

Although discovering angels in hidden, deeply personal ways is without doubt much more likely than full-blown angel sightings, and it is very rare to actually see or hear an angel, this does not mean it doesn't happen. Quite the contrary, angel sightings can and do happen, and over the years I have been fortunate to receive many letters and emails about this phenomenon. Let's start with this one from Mary.

Don't look back

Almost nine years ago, my husband, now in his mid-seventies, was in intensive care in the Victorian Infirmary in Glasgow. As I was walking up a quiet street on my way to the Infirmary I noticed that an elderly lady, or so I thought at the time, was about to pass by me on my left. I hadn't been looking at her, so didn't really notice her face until, as she was about to pass, she turned towards me: she had a pleasant face, about thirty-ish and such a beautiful smile. She passed, and I felt that I shouldn't look back. I knew I had seen an angel. Don't ask me how. I just knew.

In virtually every case when people get in touch with me to tell me about angel sightings they share the same powerful conviction, the 'just knowing', that Mary expresses here. They are in no doubt at all that what they saw and felt was real. They were not dreaming or hallucinating or imagining it. They actually saw angels.

Sometimes heaven may appear in human form, as was the case for Mary, but for others the form is dreamlike. This was the case for Linda, whose story follows on below, and as you can see it did not make the experience feel any the less real for her.

My wee tale

It happened a few years ago when I was on holiday in Tenerife with my husband and our two young children. Two or three days before flying home I became anxious but couldn't put my finger on what was wrong. I started experiencing shortness of breath and really started worrying about my state of health. I thought perhaps it was a reaction to something I'd eaten on holiday and convinced myself I had just developed an allergy to peanuts! However, as our departure approached I became progressively worse, so much so that on the night before we left, I had to sleep in the lounge of our apartment with the patio door open as I didn't want to worry my husband with my fretting and shortness of breath. It was a really horrible feeling. I really thought I might be dying. I hadn't experienced that before and haven't since.

I don't know if I was asleep or not because I was restless and couldn't get comfortable – however, an angel appeared at the bottom of the couch. I am absolutely sure she was real. I'll describe her if I may as perhaps other people have had similar experiences or have in fact met one. She was tall and well made and had shoulder-length dark bushy hair. She had white skin and the kindest face I have ever seen. She was dressed in a bright white flowing dress. She didn't have any wings that I could see, by the way. She was surrounded by bright lights and a small throng of people. Some were children and she was holding their hands. Some were men – I saw an Asian chap, for some reason he stood out. She spoke to me and said, 'Don't worry, Linda, it's not your time.' Then she smiled the kindest of smiles and I remember crying with sheer relief. She never told me her name. I just knew somehow that it was Carol.

Well, the following morning it was time to fly home. We flew into Gatwick in a thunderstorm and our plane was hit by lightning. For a minute or two there was real fear and panic in the plane; bags flew to the floor and people screamed. I was calm and smiled across at my terrified husband. I held my two kids close but knew we were going to be OK and we were.

Well, that's my story. I think Carol was taking some new souls with her to heaven – the little throng of people around her were calm. I think perhaps I'll meet her again one day, not for some time I hope, but it will be good to see her. Thanks for taking the time to read my wee tale.

Hilary sent me this account about an experience a friend of hers had.

The ice sculpture

On 29 December my friend had been awake for several hours and unable to get back to sleep. At around four in the morning he was lying in bed looking towards the window when suddenly a very bright light appeared in the middle of the curtains. It took the shape of a huge wing and looked slightly translucent, like an ice sculpture. Colours of light blue, green and white came from it and it lasted about a minute and then seemed to 'melt'. He said it was slightly scary but rather beautiful at the same time. He said he must have dropped off to sleep shortly after that. The next evening, at around nine, he was in the bedroom taking the T-shirt he wears in bed off the radiator. As he did so, all these blue lights started coming off it like electric sparks. Had the T-shirt been nylon, he would have wondered if it was something to do with that, but it was cotton. It continued to do that for a while and then stopped.

Hilary's friend is fortunate that he has been able to share his incredible experience with a sensitive and sympathetic soul like Hilary, because many people tell me that even though they are convinced what they saw was real, when they try to share it with other people they are either laughed at or told that they must have been seeing things, or that what they saw was not real. Not surprisingly, the effect this typically has is to make people reluctant to share their wonderful truth with others, which is an incredible shame. It can also make them doubt if what they saw was actually real, but as I stress in every one of my books the question of what is real and what is not real is something that has no cut-and-dried answer. Even scientists admit that there are invisible layers of existence, and who is to say that when someone sees an angel they are not glimpsing another invisible reality.

Lynn certainly believes she caught a glimpse of the heavenly. Here is her story.

The gift

I am sixty-one years old now, but when I was twenty-four years old, in 1974, I had a major breakdown and was hospitalised in north London. I had a few relapses but found myself in a bad place at home with my parents. My late father was physically abusive to me and also called me names, which I didn't need.

Well, anyway, I was in the box room – my childhood bedroom – and I was sitting on the bed, feeling very unhappy, when an orb of light appeared. It was about 4 feet off the floor and about 7 inches in diameter. It was a gold, undulating light. I was amazed and just kept looking at it, wondering what it was. I felt full of peace and tranquillity and love. It was like looking at a firework display. Now this happened before much was written about angels and since then I have read and read books to discover or try to discover what it was. I still don't know for sure, but what I do know is that it was a gift that gave me strength and hope when I most needed it and I often wonder about it even now.

Afterwards my life did gradually get better – I found a tiny bedsit to live in and rediscovered the joys of painting nature and all good things in life. I do feel the presence of angels from time to time and I think they come in many different disguises.

The theme of light and brilliance also features in this next story, sent by a lady who didn't leave an address for me to get in touch to reply to her. I hope if she is reading this book she will get in touch with me so I can thank her.

Brilliant light

My angel story happened in February 1997. My dog woke me during the night. Normally I would have just switched the light on, but this particular night, due to a chest infection, I had my back to the light switch so did not touch it. Then I realised the room was filled with brilliant light. At first I thought it was the red light from a car but I knew that would give one beam across the room. This light, however, was so brilliant, a brilliant white. I watched it over the bedclothes and saw two massive lights shining from the ceiling to the floor. One was much bigger than the other and the smaller one seemed to be trying to communicate with the larger one. I watched for a few minutes and then the room went black again. I was so inspired by the experience that I wrote this poem about it:

Two angels

Two angels visited me at night.
The room was bathed with brilliant light.
Just light as I have never seen before,
Two angels gleaming from ceiling to floor.
With no beginning and no ending.
Massive rays of light ascending.
I observed this light for a while.
Then closed my eyes, with a smile.
When next I looked the light had gone
and darkness had descended
the room was black and dark again.
Something, I could not explain.
This awesome sight, I shall remember.
Two angels, visiting in all their splendour.

Michel didn't actually see bright lights or an angel, but he is convinced he heard and felt one. I want to share his sensational story with you now.

Too hot to handle

The story that you're about to read is about the day I almost died, and I remember it as if it happened recently. It was nineteen years ago on 6 February. I was getting ready to go to work the graveyard shift from 11.30 p.m. to 7.30 a.m. at a smelter where I had worked for over twenty-seven years for a company that makes nickel. I talked to my wife Sandra and told her that I'd see her in the morning. Then

I kissed her and our two dogs, Lady and Duchess. As I was opening the door, we felt the cold air. I said goodbye and closed the door. I walked a few steps to my mini-truck, opened the door, got in very fast and started the truck. It was warm in about five to ten minutes, and then I drove off. It was about half an hour's drive to the parking lot.

When I arrived at the parking lot I took out my little tester to find out if the plug was OK to plug in my truck, because I have a block heater inside my vehicle. It was OK, so I plugged my truck to the outlet. Then I walked over to the change house so I could change from my street clothes into my work clothes. A little later, when I was ready, I put on my big parka and off I went to the building where I worked, which is about two football fields long. Also, it is where we pour hot molten nickel. It took me five minutes to get there. Once I got in, the place was empty, not a soul in sight. I thought the others might be in the lunch room but when I arrived in the lunch room there was no one here either.

I took off my parka and placed it on a hook. I grabbed a cup and made myself a cup of coffee and waited for my three co-workers: Bert, Brian and John. One of them came in not too long after that, and then the other two showed up minutes later. We talked till 11.30 and then we went out into the building. Bert told me that he would get the crane checked and then come down to the building. Minutes later, Bert came down and stopped over a row of moulds (vats). In between the moulds are troughs full of sand. Bert said, 'Mike, I can't lift the ingot [mould with cold and hard nickel], because the troughs have got sand in them.' I replied, 'Give me a minute, I'll grab a shovel and I'll be there.' Not long after that I was walking on the centre sidewalk with the shovel. As I was approaching that mould I walked onto another mould which was not covered. The crust wasn't thick enough to hold my weight. I was up to my waist in hot molten nickel. As I walked into it I heard Brian screaming, 'Mike, Mike!' I was also screaming now and I was in shock.

Then, out of the blue, I heard a voice saying, 'Mike, go to the side.' I walked over to the side in slow motion. I placed my left leg on the side, and again I heard the voice, 'Go onto the sidewalk and start rolling.' Then I felt something on my right leg as if something was lifting my right leg. Once I was on the sidewalk, I started to roll. As I was rolling, Brian stopped me and took off his working gloves and patted me to put the fire out.

Bert saw everything, so he called our boss on a two-way radio. Minutes later, I was surrounded by people from different departments. Sometime after midnight the ambulance came and took me to the hospital. I lost two months of my life. Two months later I was still on the morphine. I was in a Toronto hospital in a burns unit, and I was given a 1 per cent chance of living. In June of 1992 I was transferred here in Sudbury. Sandra and I figured out that I was in hospitals a little more than a year but I was determined to drive my truck and go back bowling. Now I'm driving a van and I'm back at work.

Well, Theresa, you're probably wondering why I'm writing to you. I read your angel books and want to know if you think an angel spoke to me. Do you think an angel came and raised my leg? I believe in angels, I read books about angels, read about stories of angels saving people and I also have two statues of angels and a key chain with an angel saying.

I wrote back to Michel to tell him that I was absolutely convinced an angel helped save his life that day. Something miraculous within and around him helped him take control of a potentially fatal situation.

Karen also believes angels were sent to protect her. She sent me this email.

An angel spoke to me

I would love to share with you two experiences that happened to me in which I truly believe that my guardian angel spoke to me! Before I do that, I just want to say that I love angels and I know they are all around us. I know that heaven has sent them to guide us, to inspire us, to guard us and protect us. Their infinite, unconditional love has helped me forever in my life and I am grateful to them.

Four years ago, I used to write a morning daily letter to my guardian angel. I could feel the presence of angels lingering around and it made me so happy. Even though I'm currently passing through a phase where I'm somewhat distant spiritually, my beliefs remain as strong as stone and I give all my worries and prayers to the angels around us. Anyway, about four years ago, around the time I used to write letters to my angel, I used to work in a company that manufactured handmade mosaics. The manager of the company was absent that day, and I was in charge. We were renovating our showroom and so it was a mess. As you entered the showroom, you would see mosaic pieces scattered on the floor, blocks of stones, sharp objects, wooden material and so on. It wasn't really a safe environment to be in.

118

Since I was in charge, it was my responsibility to close our show-room at the end of the business day. At around 6.00 p.m., after everyone had already left, it was time for me to leave as well. I was in a hurry because I had to meet my friends at 6.30 in a coffee shop. To reach the exit door, I had to pass through that messy showroom which I just described. So, I took my purse, closed my office and started walking fast to the way out. Before I reached the showroom, the electricity went off and it was so dark, I could not see anything at all — but that did not stop me from continuing to walk out. In fact, I started running. While the electricity was still off, I reached the showroom, walking in a rush; I did not want to stop. When, suddenly, something loud inside of me told me to just STOP! STOP RIGHT NOW AND DON'T TAKE ANY OTHER STEP! WAIT FOR THE LIGHTS TO COME BACK!

At this very moment, I stopped and just stood there in the dark doing nothing but waiting for the lights. I thought to myself, What is that? What just happened? As the lights came back, I looked down to see a tall and thick plank of wood filled with nails touching the tips of my shoes. If I hadn't stopped at that moment, I would have slipped down and taken a very bad fall that might have resulted in me breaking my foot or hand. Amazed, smiling, grateful and feeling the warmth of my angel around me, I jumped over that piece of wood and continued my way out safely.

Another incident happened around six months ago. It was a Tuesday morning and I had a very important report to submit at nine in the morning to my supervisor. I had prepared it during the previous day and put it in the drawer of my desk. As soon as I arrived at work that morning, I opened my purse to get my key to unlock my drawer but to my surprise, I could not find that key! I panicked and started a search for that key all over the office but it was nowhere to be found. I sat there in my chair thinking about what I should do. I took a deep breath, then prayed to heaven and to my angel to help me find a solution to open that drawer. After I finished my prayer, something got over me. In fact, I felt that something inside was 'driving' me. For some reason, I turned and opened the cabinet beside my desk. Inside, there were around two dozen keys (which I did not know what they were for) on the shelf there. Without even thinking, I randomly picked a key from that bunch and put it into my drawer's lock. Astoundingly, it opened!!! What made me turn and open the cabinet? What made me pick the right key first time from a bunch of keys I did not know what they were for? Thoughts started racing in my head. My face was warm. For a couple of minutes, my mind stood still. But I knew . . . I knew this was the work of my angel and it made me so happy! And I will be forever grateful.

This next amazing story also features the voice of an angel.

Angels can and do save lives

I am writing to you to let you know how much I have enjoyed your books, and also to tell you of a few of my angel experiences in the hope that you might be able to use them in any of the follow-up books you write about angels.

I have always believed in angels and imagined angels were with me. I have had many strange experiences in my life and I am seventy-six now; things that always make me feel someone is protecting me and watching over me.

The most dramatic incident that happened to me took place about twenty years ago. I had a German friend staying with me for a week. It was arranged through the local twinning association. Her name was Dr Kristen Packe. My friend Julia had been to stay with her in Weil am Rhein the previous year but for the return visit Julia could not manage it because she had MS and couldn't really cope with entertaining. So I said I would have Kristen to stay and take her out, that we would all go together in fact whenever I could manage it.

So one Saturday in November I decided to take Kristen, Julia and her daughter Catherine to Bosham, a picturesque sailing/fishing village the other side of Chichester, our nearest city. On our way home after a lovely day out, we were just coming up to a big roundabout that got us onto the Bognor Regis road when it suddenly seemed to go extra dark, as though all the streetlights had gone out, and then I heard a voice! It said very clearly, 'There is going to be an accident here.' I thought it was my imagination but looked carefully both ways through my car window anyway.

What I saw was that a car that had come off the dual carriageway was going much too fast overtaking another car and as it did so it just clipped that car and sent it flying up into the air while it carried on its way. I looked up and I can still remember thinking, So that's what the underneath of a car looks like, but as I was thinking that my foot was pushing down hard on the accelerator because it looked as though the car was going to land right on top of us! It actually landed, on its roof, behind us where we had been a few seconds before, then skidded across the road, demolished a brick wall and came to rest back in the middle of the road, still on its roof with petrol and glass covering the whole road.

Kristen shouted at me to stop, and it was only her voice that made me release my foot and put it on the brake instead. Kristen said, 'Quickly, I must go and see what I can do to help.' She and Catherine ran back to see what could be done while Julia and I slowly made our way back after putting the hazard lights on. The police and fire engines were there very quickly, closing the road to get it cleaned up. I imagine someone in one of the houses had phoned. The amazing thing was that the young man in the car was able to get out without any serious injuries. After Kristen had examined him and seen him into the ambulance she said, 'He had his seat-belt on which probably saved his life even though he travelled quite a way upside down.'

When we finally started our journey home, I asked the girls which one of them had told me there was going to be an accident there, the voice had been so clear, but they all three said of course they hadn't said anything like that – how could they possibly have known? I realised then that it was either my husband who had died a few years earlier or my guardian angel. Whoever it was, I thanked him or her because if I hadn't been warned, that car would have landed on top of us. There wouldn't have been any way we could have got clear and there would have been five people involved instead of just one, and who knows if any of us would have got out alive. If it was my angel I am eternally grateful, and wherever I go in the car now, long or short distances, I always ask my angels for protection and I'm sure I receive it.

Linda also believes there is an angel on her shoulder.

An angel on my shoulder

I used to live on my parents' two-and-a-half acre property after my dad passed so I could look after my mum. There was a lot of grass and we had a ride-on mower which I used all the time to cut it. Obviously, this had really big blades underneath so it had to be used with caution. When the cylinder at the side and back of the mower was full the blade had to be raised and the grass emptied.

One day I forgot to raise the blade and as I put my hand under the tube the blade hit three of my fingers. I was just too afraid to look at my hand because I was sure that my fingers had been chopped off. The pain was absolutely unbearable and I almost passed out. I sat on the seat of the mower and managed to call my husband but when I looked at my hand all that was there was a small dent in two of my fingers and they looked a little bruised. I had been sure my fingers were missing or at least that I would have a black and blue hand the next day. While I was sitting there a white feather – which in your books you describe as an angel calling card – came down from above me and landed on the bonnet of the mower. After that day I did not have one bruise or any pain in my hand at all. An angel must have been there with me.

The next story happened when I was having a particularly bad time in my life. I used to sit up worrying. One night, I was lying in bed in the dark and as I looked out of the bedroom door I saw a really bright light. It was almost as if someone had turned a fluorescent light on. We lived in a mobile home at the time and we had a large shed which had a security light on it, so I got out of bed to see if the light had come on but as I walked outside the door the strange light just disappeared. If the security light came on it was timed to stay on for five minutes and this light was so much brighter than it had been actually in the house. To this day I wish I had stayed in bed to see if the light would have come into the bedroom. It had made me feel so very calm and peaceful.

The other incident involved my husband. He is a roofer. I received the dreaded call from his business partner that he had fallen off a roof and had been taken to hospital. My children and I raced to hospital and all the way I was praying that he would be OK. As we walked into A&E the doctor and nurse came towards me and I was sure they were going to tell me he was in intensive care or worse, and by this stage I was almost unable to stand. The doctor's words to me were, 'Your husband is fine, he has a cut on his head and a graze on his shoulder, but apart from a little bit of shock he is fine and can go home.' He then said, 'By rights your husband shouldn't be here after falling from that height today, he must have had an angel on his shoulder looking after him.' I really do believe he did.

I do have many stories of help and contact from the other side, which continues to be a major comfort to me in life. I would love to think that I may be one of the lucky ones in life who get to actually see an angel, but at the same time I do realise how lucky I am that we have been so helped by the angels.

Linda wishes she could see her angels more clearly but her story shows that even though they chose to manifest themselves to her in less obvious ways they are always around her. Indeed, her angels may well have good reason for not revealing themselves more decisively because in spirit, belief without proof is the most potent force of all; it is the very definition of faith.

It is true that the great majority of people who write to me already believe in angels, as Linda so clearly does, or are drawn to the idea of them and, however unexpected or unusual, an angel experience simply strengthens their belief. However, I must stress that I also get emails and letters from people who tell me that until their heavenly encounter they did not believe, or never really thought about celestial beings, but then their lives changed beyond recognition when an angel appeared to them.

My aim so far in this chapter has been to open your mind and your heart to the very real possibility that angels are all around us, but I am aware that many of the stories I have used to make this point feature a dramatic or sensational element. Now that I have your attention I want to make it clear that celestial beings will typically prefer to make their presence known in more subtle ways. They prefer this quiet approach because it makes it easier for you to discover their true meaning and their significance to you, and by far the most powerful and healing way for angels to reveal themselves is from the inside out, rather than the outside in. For example, there may be an unexpected feeling of sudden warmth or comfort or, in times of sadness or grief, it may feel as if an invisible cloak of feathered wings is wrapping softly and warmly around you. Alexis talks about such a heart-warming sensation in this next story.

Strong wings

When I was little, about seven years old, I started having nightmares about being taken away from my home by a dark-haired man who would lock me in a house with a group of people I can only describe as a cult. Night after night they would abuse me until I would wake up screaming. I couldn't tell anyone as I was too young to understand, and I couldn't help but feel that I must be dirty in some way for this to happen in the first place.

When I was twenty-five I met through a friend a man who was a Reiki healer, and luckily he agreed to heal me. His wife was always present, which gave me a sense of calm, as you can imagine I was a bit fearful of trusting men. I found Reiki to be very calming, even though the chair I was sitting on would always seem to wobble, but on my third visit nothing short of a miracle happened.

I had just sat down and taken a deep breath when I felt beautiful strong wings surround me in a warm protective embrace. And as if that wasn't enough love, I felt my angel press his cheek up against mine, as if all he wanted me to feel was the incredible love he had for me. (I am saying 'he' but to be honest I cannot say whether my angel was male or female.) My heart was filled to bursting with the most indescribable feeling of unconditional love. The heat I felt was tremendous, like sitting right next to a fireplace. Although there was no doubt that I could feel my angel, I couldn't actually see him.

Only last month I was lying in bed meditating when I felt an angel cup my head in his hands. The angels' strength and power is astounding, but they are so gentle and loving all at the same time. I am truly blessed to have them in my life and my dreams. Since that night my nightmares have lessened, thanks to my angels.

Alexandra wrote to tell me about the gentle ways in which her angels reveal themselves to her.

Very lucky

The first experience I had was when I was about thirteen or fourteen. I don't remember exactly when because I had been going through some difficult times at that period. How to begin . . . when I was thirteen or fourteen my parents (mum and stepdad) worked from early to late and I was often left to look after the house and my two younger siblings, as well as preparing for my GCSEs. To cut the story short, one night I was sleeping over at my friend's place for the first time in my life – just opposite my house – and at around 2 a.m. I woke up hearing really loud music. When I actually woke up properly I realised that it was a classical orchestra and a choir I was hearing and it was coming from everywhere; it sounded like the whole world was singing just for me. It was so soothing I just lay there and listened till I fell back to sleep. When I woke up and remembered the sound it made me cry, it was so beautiful. I was so relaxed and calm and able to cope with all my responsibilities much better for a long time after that.

My other experience was when I was sixteen. We had moved to a different house and my parents had gone to a Christmas party and not yet returned and it wasn't like them to come back so late. It was about three in the morning and by that time I was really, really scared. I knew they weren't driving and that the trains stopped running at a certain time. I was looking out of the window for hours and wondering where they were when I saw a light flash by my eyes, very quickly. I was looking for it but couldn't see it again, then out of nowhere the light come back right outside my window and stayed there, just flying about. I couldn't move, even though I wanted to open the window. I felt a warmth and calmness flow through me even though I couldn't move. My mind went completely blank just staring at the light.

The light went again and came back after about three minutes and stayed there for about half an hour, and then this powerful force took my head and swung it to my left and I saw my mum walking in. When I turned back the light was gone. I am now twenty-two and haven't seen or heard anything like it since. I really wanted to share my experiences with you as I think it's really amazing what happened to me and I have been thanking heaven ever since.

The sound of beautiful music from no earthly source is often associated with angels and features in this next story from Kathleen.

Celestial sound

After reading your book *An Angel Changed My Life* I am inspired to tell you of one of many experiences I have had. I had just turned sixty and been made redundant from my job, but had managed to find a new job as a carer; a complete change of career. My father was in a care home in England and I wanted to gain knowledge of caring for the elderly to enable me to bring him home to stay with me. Previously I had suffered with bipolarity and was very aware of feelings of isolation, being dependent and helpless. That's why I so wanted to help my father enjoy his remaining years. I was making plans to accommodate his needs and trying to get money to fund necessary changes to my house.

It was a freezing cold night and the heater had packed up in my car, but that wasn't going to stop me from getting to my client. She would need her supper and a tuck-in. While I was driving along the new bypass to her home, the road seemed almost deserted when suddenly I heard the most wonderful sound of celestial music. I became quite disorientated and wondered where the sound was coming from. I had no sound system in my car and there were no houses on that stretch of the road either. No sooner had I heard the music than it began to fade and out of nowhere I heard a voice loud and clear say 'Keith', which is my pet name used by family and closest friends. I was absolutely mesmerised by the experience and couldn't quite understand what it was all about.

On arriving home, I got my answer. I walked towards my front door and noticed the lights were on and I knew I had not left them on. Someone had entered my home uninvited. I was wise enough to call the police and the person was arrested and charged. The ironic part was that this was someone previously homeless whom I had helped and befriended without question, but my experience made me be a little more cautious. Was I being warned and guided from above by that beautiful music?

I wrote back to tell Kathleen that I believed her angels were indeed using the medium of music to guide and warn her. I believe they chose the medium of music for Kathleen because of its ability to stir the soul and, as well as urging her to be more cautious, her angels were also reminding her to nourish her soul; to take care of herself as well as she takes care of others.

Music is again a powerful feature in this next inspiring story from Natasha.

Birthday miracle

On 22 January 2010 it was my twenty-ninth birthday and I was in a happy and contented mood. I had planned to meet up with some friends for a birthday lunch. I decided to go upstairs and wash my hair before meeting with my friends – a girl wants to look her best on her birthday.

I went upstairs and ran a bath. I was home alone that day as my little ones were at school and my husband David was at work. The house was in complete silence and I kind of liked it like that – it had been such a hectic morning seeing them off that I was enjoying the peace and quiet.

I was in the middle of washing my hair when I heard footsteps downstairs – our house really echoes. I then heard a woman's voice calling out my name several times. I thought it was my mother-in-law as she had said she would pop round that morning to drop off my birthday presents, so I called back, 'I'm coming, just one minute.' I quickly finished washing my hair and sorting myself out then dashed downstairs to meet my mother-in-law.

To my surprise, when I got downstairs I found that the house was completely empty. Baffled, I went into the kitchen and turned on the kettle to make a cup of coffee. I remember asking myself if I had imagined someone calling my name – but I knew I hadn't as it was so clear and I even heard the footsteps loud and clear.

I stood in the kitchen playing over in my mind what had just happened when all of a sudden the entire house filled with the most beautiful angelic music. It sounded like a large choir singing right in my dining room. The music was so clear and I could hear it as though there really was a choir singing in my dining room.

The music was so very beautiful that I burst into tears and could not stop crying. The music seemed to reach deep down into my very soul and pulled at each emotional string I had. It lasted a good few minutes before the house went silent again. The whole kitchen felt warm and had a lovely atmosphere in it.

After that magical experience I just stood there in my kitchen in amazement. I have never heard such beautiful music in all my life. My entire body shook and I felt an overwhelming feeling of inner peace and comfort. For the rest of the day I kept crying – happy and contented tears. It was the most wonderful birthday present I have ever had and one that I will never, ever forget. That magical experience will remain with me for all my life.

Another subtle way for angels to speak to you is through the sensation of someone standing behind you but when you turn around there is no one there. Then there is the sound of ringing in your ears. Not the harsh sound of an ear infection, or tinnitus, but a gentle high-pitched noise that lasts for a minute or so and then fades away. I always think of this as an angel downloading information to your soul. Sometimes other people will offer you hugs and comfort. Never discount the idea that your guardian angel can use other people to bring a message of love and comfort. Your angel will use whatever means it can to touch your heart. And sometimes an inexplicable presence is felt – like a sudden rush of air created by the passing by of an 'angel on a mission'. And sometimes there is no sensation at all, just a strange or unusual event coupled with a strong belief that an angel is watching over you.

This was certainly the case in this next story sent to me by Anne.

The white dove

When I look back over my life and examine the good things and the bad things I realise that even the worst things that have happened have helped me get to the wonderful place I'm at now. (Very happily married, with a lovely house, all the animals I've ever wanted and a brilliant son and two stepsons.)

That's a bit of background but there are a couple of stories I wanted to share with you and this first one happened not long after I'd read one of your books, in December 2009. I was driving to North Yorkshire (from Derbyshire) to look at a Labrador puppy (we were getting one for our family for Christmas). I was in the car on my own and going on a route I had never been on before. It was not at all scary for me as I often travel to new places on my own by car. I came to a place (unfortunately I don't know the name of it) where the road went into a single lane, between buildings (almost like creating a tunnel) and the traffic light was on red at my side. As I sat in the car I noticed (not more than 6 ft away from the passenger-side window) a white dove was sitting on the wall just staring straight at me. It was mesmerising and I couldn't take my eyes of it for what seemed ages – although I suppose it was only a minute or so. I was sitting there thinking, how strange for me to feel that a bird was actually observing me with such intent! I suddenly came back out of my 'trance' and glanced up and thought, Oh no, the light's on green and I've been sitting here like a lemon. I was just about to move forward when a massive lorry came hurtling out of the 'tunnel' at high speed.

I don't think it really dawned on me straight away, but then as I drove on I suddenly realised that if I had gone through when the light had first turned to green there was no way that the lorry wouldn't have smashed into me. I really do believe that the dove was some sort of guardian angel sent to distract me and prevent me from having a head-on crash.

A lot of people may read a story like this and put it all down to luck, but as I never tire of saying in my books, angels make a habit of appearing in the most unlikely of disguises, and there is no doubt in Anne's mind that luck had nothing to do with it – an angel saved her life. She was clearly incredibly fortunate to escape death and it is not hard to believe that a higher force was protecting her. It is also hard not to believe in this next astonishing story sent to me by Robert that there are angels on his strong shoulders.

The story of my life

This might seem like a long story but it is the story of my life and I am now a 73-year-old man who has been supported and guided by angels throughout my life.

I think it all began when I was nine or ten years old. We lived at the top of a very steep hill and on this day I was playing with my best friends – two girls and one boy – at the bottom of the hill in a stream that was close to the road when I suddenly had a powerful feeling that I must push all my friends out of the stream to the other side of a tree. I pushed them all out and at that same moment a coach came careering down the hill out of control, left the road, crossed the stream and smashed into the tree we were now behind. Mercifully we were all saved that day including the driver, who escaped with just bruises. That was my first contact with angels although at the time I was too young to realise.

Several years later I left school and became an electrical apprentice. The thought of having to be called up to National Service at eighteen years and not continue my trade training was daunting so when I was seventeen years old I volunteered to go a year earlier in order that I could ensure I would be placed in the Royal Engineers and continue my trade training.

After my basic training I was posted to Germany where I was soon not only doing electrical training but also engineering, carpentry and vehicle mechanics. I got on well with the officers and NCOs above me and within a year was promoted to lance-corporal and put in charge of the workshops. On one particular day I gave four men the task of working on an earth grader, which was a large vehicle about 10m long. They had to remove all its wheels to perform the task, with all of them working underneath. I left them to it and went to my office behind the workshop and had only been there for about ten minutes when I just knew that my men were in danger and I had to get them out straight away.

I ran round to the workshop and ordered the men out without giving them any reason why. Just as the last one left, the vehicle crashed to the ground. Not one man would have lived if I had not removed them – my angel had been with me again.

I was just twenty years old at the time and did not know yet about angels and their protection, and I thought it was just my intuition but I had a lot to learn.

Part of my duties was to guide my squadron across country to a solid ground location that was suitable to camp and support our heavy plant, cranes, lorries, tanks and so on when out on manoeuvres and this is another classic example of more angel guidance and protection in my life. On this occasion, I had used a map as usual to reach our destination, which was 400 miles from our camp, an area that I had never been before, and I had left signs along the route but was unable to locate an area to put the squadron. I also had a terrible headache and told my driver to pull over and stop for a rest. I lay down on my seat and suddenly felt warmth go through my body. In my mind I saw the way to go. I gave instructions to my driver and we arrived at the perfect location.

I believe only an angel could have given me such guidance and this guidance has continued throughout my life; wherever I was in any country I was serving in I knew what was around the corner and what an area would look like.

In all the cases above I believe the people involved tuned into their inner angel – which some may prefer to call their intuition, but to me it is their inner angel, *anam cara*. For example, if Robert had not listened to his inner angel, neither he nor his friends or colleagues would have lived to tell to the tale. Stories like this prove to me that intuition is the voice of your guardian angel speaking to you. The problem is, many of us don't trust that voice.

Today, Marysia is convinced that her guardian angel speaks

to her through the voices in her head and heart, but as you will see from her story below, she had her doubts, and it took a series of compelling incidents to change her mind.

Listen to me

I was brought up a Roman Catholic and was taught about guardian angels and I always found them a comforting thought through childhood, but as one gets older one changes and they were no longer part of my life. However, I have had lots of strange experiences and I am including some of them, and I believe they were all the work of my guardian angel.

No.1 – I was sitting on a park bench in the sunshine enjoying my lunch, away from the office, just relaxing. A young man came and sat not far from me on another bench. Immediately, the thought came into my mind, Beware – hide your handbag. There was nothing peculiar about him so I dismissed the thought. Five minutes later, he came over, stretched across me and snatched my handbag! I chased him through the park and eventually he threw my handbag into a bush and said, 'OK, OK, you can have your handbag back.'

No. 2 – Several years later, in February, I was driving to work along a very icy road and because that morning a sudden thought had come into my head about the ice, I had asked my husband what to do in case I slid on the ice. He explained about pumping the brake and not stamping hard on it. I had set off and, again, didn't worry too much. Then I actually found myself sliding towards a parked car on the ice and realised what was happening, and although I did cause some damage to the car (I left my telephone number, the car was fixed on insurance and it did cost me), without my husband's driving advice it could have been a whole lot worse!

No. 3 – Again, a driving experience. I was driving back from my daughter's, very tired, and I must have fallen asleep at the wheel of the car. Something told me to wake up and I woke up to find one of my front wheels making a very odd noise and realised I had driven into a kerb. The tyre was completely ruined, as was the wheel. However, this was on a main road – I hadn't destroyed the car, hadn't killed myself, or driven into any other car. My husband naturally was very worried – but I just don't know how I survived.

No. 4 – This last experience was a defining one. After my last two scrapes I realised it was my guardian angel looking out for me and when I was at a jewellery party, amongst the other beautiful things I bought a silver angel pendant with the words 'Watch Over Me' etched into the back. I kept this in my handbag. A friend of ours was going to have a major operation on his arteries and I was very worried about him, and a voice in my head told me I had to give him my angel. I honestly thought he would ignore it, leave it in his pocket and forget all about it, but sometime later, he came up to my husband and said, 'You must thank Marysia so much.' My husband didn't know what he was talking about – because I hadn't told him about the angel. Apparently our friend had gone into the operating theatre holding the angel and had kept it with him all the time. He made a complete recovery and is now awaiting a further op for his heart. He still keeps the angel with him all the time.

I know a lot of people would be completely sceptical, but I know I shall never ignore the voice in my head anymore. My angel obviously doesn't think my time is up yet!

I'm always apprehensive talking about voices in the head in my books because so many people associate it with madness, but as these stories show, more often than not the voices in your head have nothing to do with insanity and everything to do with divine inspiration.

We all talk to ourselves, but do you ever hear a voice in your head that you know is not your own? It is not the same as a thought. It is a loud, clear voice that guides, warns, protects, and inspires you to take action when you otherwise might not have. It is the voice of your guardian angel calling out your name.

Fourteen years ago I heard the clear voice of an angel calling my name. I was at a busy junction deciding whether to turn left or right when this voice – it was the voice of my mother in spirit – urged me to 'take the right path' and head in the direction I had not intended when I started my journey. That angel-inspired change of direction saved my life, because if I had turned left I would almost certainly have been involved in an accident that claimed three lives. Yes, I've heard the voice of an angel and although I may behave a little crazily at times, as we all do, I'm not insane. I've got all my wits about me. And, I have had many letters and emails from people who have experienced something similar warning them of danger. As far as I know, none of these people are insane either. Like me, they are normal people going about their lives, when something out of this world intervenes to change their lives forever.

The clear, calm voice of intuition is a theme in this next story, sent to me by Kathleen.

The mini-miracle

I am prompted to write of my own inexplicable 'coincidence', which happened nearly forty years ago and which I have never forgotten. It was a cool spring morning and my baby boy was only about three months old. My mother was staying with us and we were preparing to go to the shops. My mother suffered from epilepsy and often collapsed into a fit without warning. For reasons I can't explain, on that morning I did two things quite by chance that were uncharacteristic before we left. I had just bought some pram reins, and although the baby was far too young to even sit up, for some reason (all the while thinking how silly and unnecessary it was) I put the harness on my little son and attached it to the hook on the pram body. At the same time I wondered if it was windy outside and, debating with myself if it was really necessary, put the hood of the pram up to keep him warm. It was a small pram with a detachable body; very trendy at the time. The main body clipped on each end with a very large clip.

We got to the local post office and I joined a queue, leaving the pram to one side of the area but in view. My mother stood near it.

All at once I heard a crash and my son screaming and I dashed over to find my mother had fallen in a seizure and her weight had knocked the pram body onto the floor, upside down. The floor was made of marble and I knew as I rescued my baby that if I had not taken either of the two precautions that morning (which had seemed so odd to me at the time) he would have suffered I hardly dared imagine what. What a relief that he was only very frightened (as was I) but completely uninjured. He was hanging from the harness and the pram hood held him up above the floor. I truly believe his guardian angel, or mine, or both, looked after us that day. My mother recovered and was OK too, I'm glad to say. If the hood had not been raised he would still have hit the floor as the harness would not have kept his body back and, of course, without the harness in place the hood would not have prevented him hitting the floor.

It was a mini-miracle, I truly believe.

But with so many thoughts and feelings in our heads and hearts, how is it possible to know whether it is your inner angel speaking and not doubts, fears or negativity? It would be easy for me to say that when you hear your inner angel speaking the voice is clear and obvious, but if this doesn't help, here are a few guidelines. The voice of your intuition will always be gentle and calm, in contrast to the voices of fear and doubt which will be frantic and noisy. In addition, your inner angel will always be positive and encouraging. It won't try to discourage you. For example, if you are worried about something you did, your inner angel won't tell you that you failed, or that you are a loser or stupid; it will tell you that there was much to learn from the experience so you can make it a more positive experience next time. And when your intuition reaches out to you, the insight or advice you get will be very clear and simple. There won't be lots of explanations or chatter or fearful 'what ifs', there will just be a quiet knowledge of the truth without need for explanation.

Every person has a guardian angel within them that wants so much to talk to them, but most of us are just too preoccupied and sceptical to listen. If, however, we can open our minds and our hearts, like the Celtic souls in this chapter did, we can hear their subtle but powerful communications. In short, our angels can only talk to us if we are willing to open ourselves to the possibility of magic and miracles in our lives. If we can do that, they will take us gently by the hand and lead us away from bitterness, pain, fear and guilt.

Heaven is waiting for us to pause in wonder and to see the world with angel eyes. The love our angels have for us is unconditional and they will be right beside us even when all hope seems to be lost. Remember, just as you don't need to be Irish to see or believe in angels, you don't have to be psychic or perfect to be loved and protected by your angels. All you need is an open mind and a trusting heart.

Perhaps you long to see angels and think you are open to the idea but don't feel they are revealing themselves to you. If this is the case, perhaps your heart and your mind haven't really opened yet. If, however, you can rediscover your Celtic soul – and by that I don't mean visiting Ireland, I mean reconnecting with the part deep inside you that sees the world as a place of unexpected wonder – then your heart will open to let your angels in. You see, it is through your heart that your angels will first reveal themselves to you.

Of course, I'm sincerely hoping at this stage in the book that you are opening yourself to the idea of angels, but if you still feel doubts or can't quite accept it all, that is absolutely fine. Take things at your own speed and don't feel you have to make your mind up. Contrary to what many people think, when I write an angel book my aim is never to prove that angels exist or to try and convince everyone, my aim is simply to give you pause for thought. The people whose stories feature in this book are normal, sincere people who believe that what they experienced really happened, and whether you choose to believe them or not is entirely your decision. All that I ask when you are reading is to remember one indisputable fact, and that is that there is so much about our lives that we simply do not understand yet. It just isn't possible to see, hear, sense or comprehend everything that happens and, in my opinion, nothing demonstrates this more eloquently than stories of healing angels.

Angels of mercy

A significant number of stories sent to me are about angels healing people, either physically or emotionally, or both. One possible reason for this is that when we are ill or suffering in some way, our minds and hearts are more open to angels because we tend to focus most on what really matters in life, rather than the usual details and distractions. Again, whenever we talk about angel healing it is impossible to avoid asking the question why angels choose to heal some people and not others.

There are clearly things about our spiritual development which only our angels know and perhaps that is why in this life we may never understand why good people suffer. Indeed, knowing the answers in this life would be wrong because if we knew why bad things happen to good people, we might become desensitised to the suffering of others. One example that immediately springs to mind is when a woman is in labour; her loved ones are not particularly concerned when she screams in pain because they know the reason why – she is bringing a baby into the world. Just imagine a world where everybody knew why suffering takes place. We would not reach out to each other in the same way in times of need and a world without compassion, empathy and concern would be a brutal place to live. We don't want or need answers, what we need is more compassion.

Having said that, from all the stories and reports I have read – for reasons we do not and perhaps should not understand – angels do sometimes intervene or respond to prayers for help in times of crisis. It is also clear that the lives of those who have been visited by an angel of mercy have been utterly transformed as a result. The realisation that they are not alone strengthens their bodies and lifts their spirits. There is often no evidence or proof, just the dramatic recovery and personal testimony. To the person involved and their loved ones, however, belief in the healing power of heaven is so powerful that no 'proof' is required. This was certainly the case for Helen. You've already read stories in this chapter about bright lights triggering healing. Her story tells of healing in the form of vibrations and waves.

Good vibration

One day I went to see a friend but as I was not feeling very well I said I wouldn't stay. My throat hurt, my nose and eyes were streaming and I had a sore head. In fact, I felt awful. I went home and went straight to bed. I was shivering and even my teeth were chattering. I drew my legs up and lay in the foetus position with my arms wrapped round my knees. I said out loud, 'Oh God, if you could only take this freezing cold out of my body I would feel better,' and no sooner were the words out of my mouth than I felt myself being turned over onto my back, then my legs were straightened and my hands pushed down by my side. I was totally paralysed, all I could move were my eyes (funnily, though, I wasn't frightened). Then I felt a vibration and waves going from my toes to head, up and down, up and down, then a high-pitched buzz (like a wireless trying to pick up a station) and then a click.

My body went limp. I was moved onto my side and went into a deep sleep for an hour. When I woke up there was nothing wrong with me, I was completely cured. Then I had something to eat. Next day I went back to my friend, who nearly collapsed with shock at seeing me completely better, so soon.

Scot is sure angels healed his pain.

Never forgotten

Years ago when I was in my late teens I went to bed one night with this throbbing stomach ache. I woke up several times and even called my mum for comfort and advice but nothing helped. It was so painful it made me cry and then just as I was about to call 999 the pain stopped. I opened my eyes and saw something that looked like a blue and white cloud hovering over me. I was amazed but also relieved.

I knew it was an angel. I knew an angel had taken away my pain. My experience has never been repeated but it's something I'll never forget. Just thinking about it has kept my faith alive all these years.

Joy is also convinced an angel visited her when she was coming down with polio in the autumn of 1941, before the serum had been invented.

Magnificent angel

I was just nine at the time. I saw this mighty angel standing by my hospital bed. She had a white robe and golden hair and she said that she would always be with me. There was so much light coming from her that I remember putting my hands up to protect my eyes. I did get very, very ill at one point and my parents must have feared the worst but I did eventually get through the sickness with no paralysis.

While I was recovering I didn't see my angel again but I did feel her presence beside me. I've continued to sense her and I always know it is her, my angel. She kept her promise to me all these years and I've never felt alone.

Shelley definitely trusts that heaven healed her, but her healing was an emotional rather than a physical one.

Peace and calm

I've just finished reading your book and wanted to tell you what happened while I was reading it.

I had just got to the bit where you say something about the light from an angel falling upon you when (and it was a dark and gloomy day) the sun suddenly came out at such an angle that I was bathed in brilliant light where I sat, and the most wonderful feeling of peace and calm came over me. I have no doubt it was my guardian angel telling me that he was there. I have long believed in angels and longed to have some sort of connection with them (I'm constantly talking to them) and through your book I got my wish.

This next story from Hayley is interesting as it shows that sometimes we are stronger physically than we think we are. Hayley is confident that angels gave her daughter the strength she needed in a time of crisis.

Angels stepping in

On 13 July at around 10 p.m. my daughter Megan was walking home and texting me on her phone to let me know she was on her way. It is very rare for Megan to walk home alone but her friends were going to a party and she chose not to join them.

She was walking along a main road which runs parallel to a canal and she was approached by a man wearing a black hooded top and stone-washed jeans who grabbed the back of her clothing and dragged her backwards for 20–30 metres behind a bush and over a grassy verge. He then threw my daughter into the canal while he escaped with her brand-new mobile phone. It was very dark and she could not see the side of the canal or any way to climb out as there was high corrugated iron along both sides. She swam away from the position of her attacker while he ran off and found two rails along the side. She was very weak and in shock and was struggling to reach the lower rung. She started to panic as her breath quickened and she felt she had no escape. From nowhere there was a surge of energy beneath her and she reached up and caught hold not of the first rung of the bars but the higher second one. She managed to haul her body up and swing her legs over the side of the canal to escape and run for help. She has no idea what happened for her to summon such strength but I know I do. Her angels were most certainly there to help her out of a very dangerous and life-threatening situation and I thank them from the bottom of my heart.

Thought you would like to hear this story . . . Megan is cut and bruised and has damaged the tendons in her left thigh and her breathing is still very erratic through shock, but I know this could have been a very different story if the angels had not stepped in.

I adore reading stories like these about angels sending feelings of comfort, hope, healing and strength to those in need, often when they least expect it. More often than not these feelings are so powerful and overwhelming that bodies and hearts are healed as a result. Don't think that the stories you have read in this chapter are the extent of it. There really is no limit to the ways in which angels can reach out to us, because they love to reveal themselves in unexpected and unusual ways. For example, while Helen was grieving deeply for the loss of her grandmother, which followed the loss of several other beloved family members, she received comfort and strength in the most unexpected place – the restroom.

Don't cry

I cried so hard I nearly choked; I couldn't stand the grief. I went to the restroom to be alone in the hospital and as I stood at the window watching the rain and sobbing my heart out I swear I heard the toilet roll turn as if Nan was offering me tissue and telling me not to cry.

I hope Helen's story, and indeed all the stories in this chapter, has shown you that angels don't just hover around sacred sites or places of worship and that they don't necessarily appear when and where we expect them to. They are full of surprises and can be found all around us and deep within us, in any place and at any moment. Sure, there are locations, like Ireland, where the veil between this life and the next appears to be thinner, but angels don't restrict themselves to specific locations. There aren't any set ways for them to appear either. Bright lights and white figures are well reported, but for you the experience may be entirely different. You should always expect the unexpected as far as your angels are concerned, and if you keep your mind open in this way, you are far more likely to discover angels anywhere and everywhere in deeply personal ways, just as the ancient Celts did all those centuries ago.

The presence of angels can be felt in every atom of creation. They are part of the interaction between all things visible and invisible, which only those with open minds and hearts or Celtic souls can see. In the next chapter you will see how this eternal truth also applies to the spirits of departed loved ones, those who have passed over to the other side. In the strictest sense angels and spirits are not the same, in that angels are pure spiritual beings who have never lived on earth. Sometimes, though, beings of light may choose to reveal themselves through the spirits of loved ones, unconsciously or consciously guided from above, and that is why I like to use the words spirit and angel interchangeably in my books.

Just like your angels, those who have crossed over to the other side are never far away from you. And, just like your angels, they can be found in everything that is loving and good and in all that gives your life meaning and hope.

CHAPTER FIVE

The Land of the Young

When we lose someone we love it seems that time stands still. What moves through us is a silence . . . a quiet sadness . . . A longing for one more day . . . one more word . . . one more touch . . . We may not understand why you left this earth so soon, or why you left before we were ready to say goodbye, but little by little, we begin to remember not just that you died, but that you lived. And that your life gave us memories too beautiful to forget. We will see you again some day in a heavenly place where there is no parting. A place where there are no words that mean goodbye.

Irish funeral prayer

Never are we more in need of spiritual guidance, comfort and healing than when a loved one dies and we find ourselves staring death in the face. Nothing brings more focus than the shadow of death. People who have never believed in angels find themselves wondering if there is an afterlife, or if their loved ones live on in the afterlife. And then there are those who have always believed in an afterlife but find doubts creep in when death, the great unknown, approaches. Once again we can learn so much here from Celtic souls. As the stories you will read here show, they don't believe in death – because they know better.

Beautiful and alive

There is little doubt that the ancient Celts believed in an after-life. In chapters two and three you saw how they believed the spirits of departed loved ones were always close by. One of the names associated with the afterlife in Celtic spirituality includes my personal favourite – the Land of the Young. Everything in this land was said to be beautiful, bright, alive and colourful. It was called the Land of the Young because in this paradise the ageing process is reversed, so the youngest are the wisest. Time has no meaning and everyone's soul longs for this wonderful place, which is more like a dream world than a land for the dead.

The Land of the Young reminds us of the close association that exists between children and heaven. Like all those who see the world with angel eyes, children don't believe death exists either, and I have received many letters and read many reports from all over the world that talk about children who see angels prior to death, whether they are dying themselves or witnessing or hearing about the death of someone else.

Celtic souls share with children this clear awareness that the grave is not the place where those who have died remain. Like children they don't have inhibiting barriers of fear and are willing to suspend their disbelief and trust what they feel and see.

Sometimes they are able to tell us what heaven looks like, but more often than not they catch glimpses of a world of brightness far more beautiful and alive than this one. They talk of miraculous things like being surrounded by light, music, celestial beings and the spirits of departed loved ones.

Perhaps nothing illustrates this better than a conversation I had with a 6-year-old boy some ten years ago now. I remember our chat so clearly. The child was the son of a close friend of mine whose father had recently died. My friend was absolutely distraught as she had been extremely close to her father. She was a single mum and I spent a lot of time with her in the months following her father's death. On one occasion I could tell she needed some time on her own so I suggested taking her little boy out for the day. I took him to the zoo and we had a brilliant time. On the way home we passed the cemetery where his grandfather was buried and I asked him if he would like to lay some flowers for him. This little boy told me quite firmly that this would be a waste of time and money because only a tiny part of his granddaddy was under the ground and the rest of him was 'hovering'. Intrigued, I asked him to explain further and I shall never forget the look he gave me – it was one of such boredom, and frustration that I didn't understand. Sighing, he told me that a tiny bit of his granddaddy was in the cemetery but obviously the rest was alive and following him and his mum around all the time.

Later that day I told my friend what her son had told me and it brought tears to her eyes. She told me that many months before her father's death, when he was still alive but terminally ill with cancer, her son had told her that she should not be upset because he could see angels all around his grandfather. He also said that he could see his grandfather's body of light and it was healthy and young. His words had been a huge comfort at the time and continued to comfort her now.

Here's another story, about a 9-year-old girl called Sally who also reassured her parents when death approached. Although she was terminally ill she would often comfort her father and mother with her powerful belief in the afterlife, a place where death, disease, pain, old age and unhappiness simply did not exist. Here's a part of the letter Sally's mother sent me. It's brief but heartbreakingly beautiful.

Singing flowers

I'm very happy. I saw the angels again today when I fell asleep. They took me to a place where it was so warm. All the flowers were singing and the trees were laughing and I got to play in the sand with lots of other children. I love it when I fall asleep because I can be with my angels and it is never cold or painful. I'd miss you, Mum and Dad, but sometimes I would like to go to sleep forever so I can play with the other children all the time and hear the flowers singing.

What a wonderful metaphor for heaven 'singing flowers' is. There is a powerful sense in this story that even when she was alive, Sally was already living in the Land of the Young. Of course, it is not just children who see angels when death is close by. People of all ages and cultures have written to me to tell me about this phenomenon. It seems that death makes children of us all.

One of the most commonly reported phenomena is seeing an angel or departed loved one or glowing lights hovering beside a dying person before they pass away. Such deathbed or parting visions can occur months, weeks, days or moments before or after a person slips away, but whenever or however they occur they are always a source of great comfort.

Janette believes she saw her mother-in-law's soul leave her body.

Beautiful gift

I would very much like to tell you about my mother-in-law. She was born in London, and was a devoted Catholic. She was called Rachel.

She had a very hard life. She was crippled, registered deaf and blind, and was a tiny woman of 4 ft 11, but she had a character as big as a mountain. When she became unable to care for herself properly, we brought her to live with us, but eventually she had to be placed in a nursing home when she got dementia. Whenever my husband and I visited her, we would both hold her hand and at some point she would always let go of her son's hand and put it in mine.

One day I went with her friend Maureen to see her. My husband stayed at home as he wasn't feeling very well. Just before we left, Maureen took some cups back to the kitchen and I bent down to give Rachel a kiss on the forehead as usual. This time she reached out and held my face in her hands, pulled me close and looked at me. I don't know why but I knew this was going to be the last time she would see me on this earth and I would see her.

From then on, every time we visited her eyes were shut. I would beg her to open her pretty blue eyes but they remained shut. On the morning she passed over we walked into her room and one of her eyes was open. This was typical of her sense of humour. It was like she was winking at us. I sat with her for a while and talked to her and then I told her son that his mum needed her last rites. The priest came and I sat and watched and held her hand. As I sat with her I saw her soul leave her body. It hovered about a foot above her, stayed for a second and then rolled into many different beautiful colours and vanished.

It was such a beautiful gift that I was allowed to watch and one I will never, ever forget.

Sue talks about the immense moment someone she loved died.

The moment

As I read your book more and more I believe that several things have happened in my life that I cannot explain.

My story starts in 1998 when my husband Paul and I split. It was a very sad time for me and I regret it so much. Paul had an affair with a friend (still not sure if it was ever a full-blown affair) and I found that I just could not forgive him.

We split, as I say, in 1998 and I didn't have any contact with him, even though my daughter Donna did, and her children. Donna was from a previous marriage and Paul looked on her and her children as his own. Donna would tell me he was depressed and wanted us to get back together again, but I would not entertain the idea. However, as time passed the anger stopped and we began to talk. We even spent days out just enjoying each other's company. In February 2000 Paul went up to Wales to help my sister who had lost her own husband. He was going to do some decorating for her. I could not join them as I had commitments at home. I spoke to Paul several times but our last phone call ended with an argument. Being stubborn I would not ring and say sorry. I only wished I had, as my sister rang me and said she could not wake Paul, and she had rung an ambulance.

I rushed to the car but knew it would take me at least four hours to get there. I didn't really know what to think as I was driving, but I was getting impatient with other drivers, and then my worst nightmare, traffic jams.

It took me six hours to get there and when I arrived my dad said that Paul had had an aneurysm and he was on life support. We rushed to the hospital, which took another hour and a half as it had now started to thunderstorm. I was beginning to think that perhaps I should not be going, as everything seemed against me. When I finally arrived Paul was just lying there, and they told me the outcome was not good. I talked to Paul all through the night, told him how much I loved him and that we could put everything behind us. I was told that he could hear me. The doctors arrived at ten the next morning and told me Paul was brain-dead.

I gave permission to have his machines turned off and I held him as he took his last breath. As Paul did so a streak of sunlight came through the window and went no further than Paul's bed. No one else saw this light – it seems only I did. As it touched Paul he squeezed my hand.

It was so strange to see and feel this sunshine/light, as it was raining outside and anyone who knows Wales knows that they get a lot of rain. Remember also that it was February and cold. I did mention it to the priest who came about his funeral and he just said that it must have been my imagination. I know what I saw and I know it happened. To this day I have wondered if this was the moment someone came for Paul and he left this earth. What do you think?

I wrote back to Sue to tell her that I have read many similar stories of people noticing shafts of light or unexplained sunlight at the exact moment of death and I was convinced this was a message of comfort and hope from the other side. I also told her that the love she shared with Paul could not be broken by death and Paul knew this when his moment came.

Lena sent me this next moving story, which is all about the healing and uplifting effect death can have.

Never forget

I have had an experience that I will never ever forget for as long as I live. It was in 1997 and my husband John was dying of cancer (it ran in his family and a few years before we had lost his sister of a brain tumour at the age of twenty-six.) We had moved our bed downstairs as that's where the bathroom was and John's strength was going. His younger brother was staying with us as was my mum, both giving me support but I was on autopilot. I have shortened this story just to tell you what I saw.

It was in the early hours of Saturday 12 July and we were both asleep when I suddenly woke up. As I turned to face John I saw a grey/silver/white mist at the foot of the bed but it was only on his side of the bed. At first I thought it was because I didn't have my glasses on and I went back to sleep. I woke up again at about 7 a.m. when John sat up straight and said he felt sick. I helped him move to the side of the bed and got a bucket but he just went all limp. I held him up as best I could and shouted for my mum and his brother to help. My mum arrived first and held him and then his brother rushed over and we laid him back down on the bed. I rang the doctor and he came straight away. I told the doctor I thought he might have something stuck in his throat but the doctor told me it was his last breath I could hear. John died at 9.30 a.m. on 12 July 1997.

A few days later when I was back in our room I was writing John a letter. I wanted to put into writing how much I loved him and as I was writing I felt a soft breeze. I just knew it was him letting me know he was OK, and although I missed him terribly I was OK because ever since I saw the mist the night John died I have felt peace deep inside me, and no matter how stressed or angry things get around me, my inside is calm.

Every person who has lost a loved one dreams of being able to communicate with them. The stories here show that this is not an impossible dream. I have received hundreds of letters and emails from readers telling me that signs from the afterlife are a reality and that they feel closer than ever to loved ones that have passed over. Yes, they tell me about feelings of intense grief and loss that their physical relationship has died but they also talk of feelings of overwhelming love, comfort and warmth as they awaken to the reality of a new and eternal relationship in spirit. This next story from Jenny says all this far better than I can.

The next room

I have definitely had experiences of afterlife communication, one of which involved a passage in a book that I read one night when I was very worried and stressed out about something that was happening the next day. The passage in the book quoted something my nan used to say to me when she was alive. Many years ago, she would say to me occasionally, 'When my time comes, if you ever want to talk to me, I'm only In the next room.' The passage in the book said, 'I have only slipped away into the next room.'

I can't tell you how reassuring this was to me. I was texting a friend about it at the time, who told me it was definitely a sign. I believe it was and the next day, the event I'd been worrying about turned out fine. Strangely enough (or not), just prior to the event, I felt a sudden and unexpected calm come upon me and somehow I knew it was going to be fine. My friend who came with me that day to advocate for me actually said that she had felt the same unexplained calm come upon her too and that she also knew it would be fine. All this suggests to me that my nan is looking out for me.

Anne wrote and told me that she also believes her mother in spirit is looking out for her.

Coming back

I'm not normally the type of person who shares experiences I have had with anyone other than my closest friends but I just know I have to share this with you.

My mother was someone who not only loved her children, she worshipped and adored us! When the grandchildren arrived she loved them so much it probably hurt. My mum died after an injury to her ankle would not heal; infection was travelling up her leg and the decision was made to amputate the leg in an attempt to save her life. Sadly, after amputation my mum never really regained consciousness and died six weeks later in hospital. I was pregnant at the time of my mum's death and gave birth to my second daughter five months later, and my third daughter two years after that.

Whenever friends spoke about people 'coming back' to visit I would always tell them that if it was possible my mum would be back to see her grandchildren, and I believe she did just that. One night, my husband was working the night shift and my oldest daughter was in bed in her own bedroom. My middle daughter – who was born after Mum died – was in bed with me lying to the left of me, and my newborn baby daughter was in her cot, which was to the right of me. I awoke and, with my eyes wide open, saw my mum standing at the foot of my bed. She was wearing a dressing-gown that I remember her wearing when I was primary school age. She walked around the bed to the side of my middle daughter, gently pulled back the quilt and said, 'She is beautiful,' before gently replacing the quilt. I lay paralysed as she repeated the exact same thing, walking around the bed to the side of my baby's cot, lifting the quilt and saying, 'She is beautiful.' All the time she was with me I was totally paralysed. I tried to speak to tell her I love her but I could not move a muscle or utter a sound.

That was twenty-six years ago and I was not dreaming at the time. I often feel that my mum is around me.

Here is what happened to Natasha.

The visit

When I was fifteen I was lying in bed asleep when I was awoken by the feeling of being watched. I glanced up towards the window and my heart stopped as there was a slim man there whose face looked very familiar. He smiled at me and placed his hand on the windowpane, as though he wanted to come in. I woke up my mother and asked her if she too could see the man standing in the window. She said no and told me to go back to sleep as I had been dreaming. About ten minutes later I had the same feeling of being watched. I opened my eyes and the same man was kneeling down beside me. He had his arms crossed, leaning on the bed with his head rested on his arms, and he was watching me sleep. When I looked at him he smiled down kindly at me and just watched me.

I sat up with a jerk and screamed out loud, waking my mother for the second time that night. I told her what had happened and she said she was taking me to see the doctor. About a month later my mother and I were looking through some old photographs that were stored away and I came across a photo of a young man.

I recognised him straight away as the man who had visited me. I asked my mother who the man in the picture was and she said it was my father when he was in his early twenties. My father had died when I was very young. She was in disbelief when I told her that he was my mysterious night-time visitor and said that I must have seen the picture before and just remembered it. I knew that I had never seen that picture before. I know now that it was my father visiting me to say he was OK and keeping well.

When someone we have a deep connection with dies it can feel as if the colour and joy in life has dried up, but then something incredible happens to fill us up again. For Anne and Natasha in their stories above, it was a vision from the world of spirit, but for others it can be something deeply personal, like hearing a familiar tune at just the right time or just a sense that the loved one in spirit is around you. This next account, sent to me several years ago now by Celia, illustrates beautifully this theme of angelic comfort and healing through the spirits of the departed.

Best friend

My brother was my best friend. Sure, we fought a lot as siblings do, but he knew I loved him dearly. When he passed away at the age of seventeen, after getting hit by a motorbike on his way to the shops, I felt as if I had lost my right arm. I wasn't sure how I could function without him. We had been so close. Being two years younger I had always looked up to him and assumed he would always be there for me. He was the best brother I could wish for.

The Land of the Young

I was six months away from taking my GCSEs when he died and I lost all passion for learning. I couldn't see the point of qualifications. My brother had done really well in his GCSEs, all A stars, As and Bs, but none of that hard work mattered now. All that time spent studying he should have spent having fun, he should have spent living. My parents begged me to get my head down but I was not the slightest bit interested anymore. I just couldn't see the point.

About three months after my brother's death, I was awakened one night by a very bright light. It was so intense I had to shield my eyes. I sat up in bed and saw the white light land on the floor and within moments it started to get bigger and bigger until it seemed to fill the whole room. Then out of the light I saw my brother. He looked incredible, so happy and relaxed. I wanted to reach out to him but I couldn't move or talk. It didn't matter though because we talked to each other through our thoughts. We talked about Mum and Dad and my brother told me I was making it very hard for them. Their hearts were breaking up and they were so worried about me. I told him that I thought qualifications were a waste of time. He laughed and said he understood because where he was none of that mattered but while I was on earth I needed to play the game. I needed to make Mum and Dad proud and I needed to make myself proud. I needed to learn and grow. If I dropped out of school now I would stop moving forward and if I stopped moving forward everyone – Mum and Dad and him – would also stop moving forward. This wasn't just about me.

We 'talked' some more and I told my brother how much I missed him and he told me that he would always be there for me when I needed him. He said some more but I couldn't make out what it was because he was starting to melt into the light. Eventually there was just the glowing ball of light left. It lingered for a while and then went out and my bedroom was completely dark again.

I sat there in bed, dumbstruck. Was it possible that my brother had visited me to help me through my grief and to let me know he was doing just fine in the light and he would never really leave me? I didn't sleep at all that night. I stayed wide awake. I knew it wasn't a dream. My brother had come back to tell me to stay on at school.

I don't think my parents will ever understand why I made the decision to stay on at school because I never told them about my vision. I don't think they would have believed me. It was the best decision I ever made. I didn't get ten GCSEs like my brother and I didn't get his high grades but I got enough to stay on for sixth form and then go to university and have the best time of my life.

I'm twenty-five now with a well-paid job in advertising. I haven't had any more visions or communications with my brother but I just know he is always close by watching over me. To this day I can recall every detail of my vision. It is as clear today as if it had just happened. I shall never forget it.

Mona will never forget her experience either. Here is her story.

Reflection

I am writing to you all the way from South Africa to tell you that I was drawn to your book *How to See Your Angels*. I found it very comforting and uplifting as I am on my own spiritual path and I constantly talk to my angels. They have really been my best friends during difficult times. They send me many signs such as feathers, stars and rays of light, and I sometimes get a glimpse of an angelic presence around my bed when I'm sleeping. The first time was about two months after my father died and I was in such distress. I felt like my world was falling apart so my mother bought me a kitten to comfort me. The kitten got sick and, after many tests, we didn't know what was going to happen. Then one night I remember closing my bedroom door before I went to sleep like I usually do. I woke up very suddenly to see the door open and my father standing at the end of my bed. I could see the reflection of the glasses that he always wore. He was in a blue aura of light and he didn't say anything, just moved around my bed towards me and gave me a kiss. The very next day my kitten was his old self again and totally cured. That was the deepest angelic moment for me.

Sue believes she has been visited in spirit by her brother.

Radiant

I believe our loved ones are always around us and they try hard to communicate with us.

When my brother was dying of cancer, I was refused early retirement from teaching. I was trying to retire on health grounds. My brother died in March 1995. In July 1995 I had a dream in which my brother came into my bedroom and walked around to me. He put his hands either side of my face and smiled. To say he looked radiant is an understatement, he looked better than anyone could in this life.

The next day I had a letter and phone call to confirm my retirement. My brother had come to tell me.

Robert, whose account follows next, also experienced a profound angelic moment.

Lost time

When my father with whom I had been so close died after a long illness at the early age of sixty years I was very upset. One day I was lying on my bed with my eyes closed wishing he was here when suddenly I felt a presence in the room and opened my eyes to see my father standing there. There was not any light around him or anything different. It was just him and we were able to talk to one another.

I also want to tell you about something else. As we did before his death, my wife and I would visit my mother every weekend and on this visit seven weeks after my father's death my mother was making a pot of tea when she said, 'Do you know what, the other day I was only saying to your father – ' Then she put her hand over her mouth and said we would think she was mad now, but I said I didn't because I had been talking to Dad too. My mum then said that my father would come to her, sit on the arm of her chair with his arm round her and they would talk.

Three weeks later I was in a meeting at work when I had a powerful feeling that my father had gone to the other side for good and would no longer be there to be called on and I was right. The next time I visited my mum her first words were that she also thought my dad had gone now.

When my mother died thirty-seven years after my father I hoped I would contact her as I had my father but she did not come through, and I had a warm feeling that she was at last back with the man she so clearly loved and was making up for lost time.

Like my father I have never been religious because looking at the world so many lives have been lost and so much damage has been done in the name of religion – and it still continues today – but I do have a strong belief in angels and the afterlife and I cannot understand why people cannot live in peace and spirit with one another.

Louise has had a number of mind-blowing encounters with her grandfather in spirit.

I see them

I have just finished reading *An Angel Changed My Life* and felt compelled to write to you. Although my family are Jewish, I have always been a Spiritualist and as a child I saw many spirits and my best friend was a spirit who spent a lot of time with me and I made my parents set a place at table for my best friend, even though they could not see anyone there.

When I was young I lived with my grandparents. My father and grandmother were fishmongers. They left for market and their shop in the early hours of the morning and the district nurse called every day around breakfast time to give my grandfather his daily insulin injection. He would potter about and give me my breakfast before my mum got up in the mornings, as she was always busy with my younger sister. My grandfather and I became very close and I can remember praying for him to live long enough for me to leave school and look after him. Sadly he died while I was still quite young.

Many years later when North Sea oil was produced and all gas fires had to be converted to take the new gas supplies I had the most incredible experience. One night as I was dropping off to sleep my grandfather appeared at the end of my bed and told me to beware of the gas fire tomorrow. This was on the day that the engineer was coming to convert our fire. At the time, we lived on the top floor of a block of flats four storeys high with a flat roof but no access to it. The front door opened onto a long hall and the kitchen opened off the hall and had a back door leading to the outside staircase. Beyond the kitchen there was the lounge and then a circular hallway with the two bedroom doors, a toilet and bathroom and airing cupboard.

I told my sisters not to leave the fire on as it was not very cold that day. It subsequently turned out that the part fitted by the engineer was faulty. If the fire had been left on, it would have exploded and my sisters would have been burned alive in their bedroom because they would not have been able to get past the lounge to the front or back exits. My grandfather could not have appeared to anyone else in the family because they would have been so afraid of seeing a ghost and would not have listened to his very important message.

What struck me afterwards was that if you had asked me to draw a picture of my grandfather the day before I saw him, I would not have been able to do so. I saw him clearly at the end of my bed, surrounded by white light (head and shoulders only). My younger sister was always a poor sleeper and we had blackout curtains, so the bedroom was in total darkness when I saw him and he had been dead for over ten years at the time.

Many years later, my mum's sister was dying of cancer and her only wish was to die with dignity in her own home. My mum and my aunt's two daughters took turns living with her and looking after her. All I could do was send her absent healing from afar. She lived on the south coast and we lived in north London at the time and I was working and had no paid holiday I could take. I offered to take unpaid holiday but my mum and cousins refused my offer of help. I knew they were all heading for a nervous breakdown and prayed for help for all of them.

One night as I was dropping off to sleep my uncle appeared at the end of my bed (same blacked-out bedroom) and told me to stop worrying because it would all be over by tomorrow. I thanked him and fell asleep and the following day at lunchtime my mum rang me at work. She started to say she had some sad news when I stopped her and said, 'Yes I know.' She said my aunt had just died, so how could I know? I said because Uncle George had told me the night before and all she could do was say, 'Oh!' – my uncle George was my aunt's husband and had died about eight years before.

Again, if you had asked me to draw a likeness of Uncle George the day before I saw him I would not have been able to do so. Yet I saw him quite clearly, surrounded by white light and again only head and shoulders in the blacked-out bedroom I shared with my sisters.

Lorraine also experienced a parting vision, and her experience happened at the exact same moment her grandmother died, even though they were apart at the time.

169

The same time

I would like to tell you about the experience I had about twenty years ago, when my grandmother died. I was the eldest of twelve grandchildren and had always been very close to her. I was staying with friends as it was New Year. My grandmother had developed bronchitis and had been taken into hospital for observation. On the night in question I was having trouble getting off to sleep. I looked at the bright red digital numbers on the clock and it said 1.24 a.m. I then sat up on the side of the bed facing the window. My grandmother came through the window. I didn't see her, I didn't feel her, but I knew she was there. It was very comforting and I was able to go to sleep. The next day we received a call to say my grandmother had died at the time she came to me. I knew then she had come to say goodbye to me. I have never felt her presence since. This experience proved to me that there is definitely something else after death.

Remember, spirits of the departed are not angels as such – because angels are spiritual beings that have never lived on earth – but sometimes angels can reach out to us through the spirits of departed loved ones consciously or unconsciously guided from above. Marilyn's story, which follows on now, says this better than I can ever explain.

Home to stay

Reading your book *An Angel Changed My Life*, I realised that what I called the spirits of my mother and grandma can also be called angels, and I believe they are. My eldest daughter, my mum (before she died) and I all saw my grandma in spirit but it is my mum I want to tell you about.

I had saved for a long time to go abroad and see my mum's sisters and brother and the cousins I had never met, but just before I went away my mum was admitted to hospital. Although she had been given the all-clear a few months before, she had a terminal illness and we feared the worst. The day before I was due to fly, the consultants said she would be OK and home by the following week. My mum knew how hard it was for me but told me to go and break the news to her siblings in person, so I went.

Every day my children phoned with an update and things seemed better. My mum was up, eating and had showered. Then In the middle of the night the call came. I was across the other side of the world and my mum had died. I felt awful and guilt-ridden for months, bereft that my mum and best friend had left me and that I had deserted her when she needed me.

Then about six months after she died I had a dream. In my dream all the family were at the airport to pick up my mum and dad. We found my dad but couldn't find my mum. We looked and looked and then a voice said, 'But Mum won't be here, she's dead.' Then a cartoon plane flew across the sky and waving at the window was my mum. She said, 'Don't worry, I'm home now. I'm sorry I've been so long, I've been on holiday with my family, but I'm home to stay now.' As this was happening I could feel all my guilt and anger and the horrible feelings about my mum's death melt away. I felt protected and warm, in a glow, and woke up smiling. I still regret going away but no longer feel guilt, just warmth when I think of Mum.

Then two years ago, after having two boys, my daughter had a longed-for girl. It was a difficult birth but thankfully both were OK. I had wished openly that my mum could have seen her great-grand-daughter and a couple of days later was babysitting my new grand-daughter. There was no one in the room but me on the settee and the baby in her rocking crib, swaddled in a blanket, days old and fast asleep. Then as I thought about my mum the crib started to gently rock and did so for quite a few minutes.

When I was alone with my daughter I mentioned this to her, and she said it had happened to her too when she was alone in the room and also that the baby would often stare into the corner of the room and smile and gurgle as if talking to someone. We both felt this was Mum, but don't know why. As I write this, a new birth is imminent and I wonder if this little boy will be visited by his great-grand-mother too. It would be nice to think so.

Psychologists are quick to argue that experiences like those Marilyn talks about in her story above are simply the grieving mind's attempt to ease the pain of loss, but if this was the case why doesn't everyone who has lost a loved one have simi-lar comforting experiences? Not everyone reports them. Also, when someone dies the immediate feelings are of loss, anger, guilt and intense pain, and feelings of comfort and healing are unlikely to occur so early on in the mourning process.

Sometimes our departed loved ones will choose to speak to us through dreams and through meaningful signs of great personal significance. This is as good a place as any to put this next story sent to me by Elizabeth.

172

Good advice

I have been reading your books on and off for the last few months and find them really inspiring. I can relate to many of the stories in them and have, I think, experienced things similar to many of your contributors. The reason I'm writing today is that something happened to me last night that I really wanted to share.

I'm quite prone to depression and treat it a little like getting a cold – some bouts are worse than others and some last longer than others but they all seem to pass. Last night I had a really rough night after working till late, having a nasty argument with my partner and, I have to say, I fell asleep exhausted after crying much of the evening. My dad passed away in 2004, and sometimes I really miss him and his good advice . . . anyway I was in a dream about nothing in particular, although I remember there was an ex-boyfriend in it and his family, when suddenly my dad appeared totally out of the blue. I exclaimed, 'Dad!' in delight and surprise and gave him a huge hug. I remember he said to me, 'I'm getting used to this now,' and then he said, 'I heard you wanted to see me' . . . I feel sure he was there to comfort me after my horrible evening. What I would like to ask you is what you think he meant by, 'I'm getting used to this now' – I think he meant he was getting used to appearing when he feels he needs to, as it's not the first such dream I've had about my dad.

I wrote back to Elizabeth to tell her that her instincts about her dad were right and he was getting used to his new life in spirit. I think he wanted his daughter to know that he was always close by however lonely and hard things felt for her. Sue also believes her mother in spirit spoke to her through her dreams. Here is her intriguing story.

Juggling

I have just started to read your book *An Angel Spoke to Me* and it's brought back many memories of when I was a child. I lost my mother at a very early age and my brother, sister and I were brought up by our nan. I always felt loved but sometimes my nan was poorly and my sister and I would be sent to stay at a children's home.

One of the dreams I had then I can still remember vividly, as though it was yesterday. I had it one night when we were in a children's home in the late 1950s and all the older girls were playing what they called 'two balls'. This is a game when you use two balls up against a wall. Many rhymes were said as you played, and what the balls were doing had to match the words of the rhyme. Anyway I could not get the hang of playing and was very upset as they all made fun of me (I was about five years old) – even my sister who was eighteen months older laughed. I went to bed crying. I still remember the dream I had that night and in it I was playing 'two balls' like an old pro. I felt wonderful.

The next morning after breakfast we all went outside and lo and behold I took the two balls and started playing just like in my dream. I could not believe it and nor could the other girls. Something so simple yet so wonderful made me feel so warm and loved. I often wonder if this was perhaps my mum's way of showing me I could do anything I put my mind to in life and not to give up.

A powerful dream convinced Gwen that her beloved great-aunt is with the angels.

Going home

When I was twelve years old my great-aunt Sarah lived opposite us. Every Wednesday she used to visit her sister – my grandmother. One Tuesday night I had a dream.

I dreamt my great-aunt stood in front of a crowd of angels. The next thing, she walked towards the angels and disappeared among them. The next day was her usual weekly visit to my grandmother's but at the end of the road my great-aunt felt unwell and had to sit down on a summer seat. Three days later my great-aunt died. I have no doubt in my mind that Great-Aunt Sarah went home with the angels. My dream was a premonition that the angels came for her.

Night visions also feature in this account sent to me by Wendy.

Golden uniform

I have just read your book *An Angel Spoke to Me*; I just had to write to you. When I was fourteen I lost my dad, who had a heart attack. The morning he died, he cuddled me and said goodbye. I think he knew he was going to die. Three weeks later it was Easter and I had a dream. My dad was in my bedroom, dressed in the same clothes he died in, and he said he had a message for me to give my mum and it was that I had to tell her she must sleep upstairs and not be afraid. She was sleeping downstairs at the time; perhaps there were too many memories upstairs. I told my mum about the dream and she decided to sleep upstairs. When she did she also had a dream that my dad was in a golden uniform and he told her he was a messenger from heaven.

Another wonderful dream story here; this time it is from a lady called Zoe.

A story of hope

I have just finished reading your book and felt that I should write and tell you about a dream I had about seven years ago now in which I believe I was visited by my guardian angel. I have always been sure that it was real as the dream was so vivid and I have remembered every detail – this is confirmed as generally the case in your book.

At the time of my dream I was staying with my mum and step-father and had been through a difficult divorce. I was drinking too much and behaving erratically. Basically I was in a bad place. I don't actually remember falling asleep but I became aware that I was walking the streets near my home and of them being covered in snow or ice that crunched as I walked. I felt somehow unsure of myself as it was dark yet light because the houses around me were covered in sparkling snow or ice. As I walked past the end of a particular street I noticed quite far up it a young man dressed completely in white, with a pure white dog at his side.

Within a second the man and dog were in front of me and I was momentarily unnerved. I asked who he was and at this point I noticed the light shining from behind his eyes and when he opened his mouth to speak the light that shone out was amazing. He then said, 'I am the one who looks after you. I am the one who makes sure you are all right.' And with that I had the sensation of being lifted up and taken back to my bedroom where he floated above my bed before I woke up. I didn't feel at peace or elated but I knew something special had happened. And although it took a while for my life to settle I truly believe he was telling me that he was keeping an eye out for me while my behaviour was so unpredictable. In the last year I have started to embrace angels and my life has definitely taken a turn for the better. And your book has given me the one thing I need more than anything . . . hope!

We have thousands and thousands of dreams over the course of our lives and the great majority of these dreams are not messages from the other side but symbolic messages from our unconscious. I'm often asked how you can tell if a loved one has actually appeared or if it is just a dream. My answer is always the same. If you wake up and the dream feels incredibly vivid and real, as it was for Zoe in her story above, and years later you can still remember it in detail and feel comforted by it, then you had a night vision and it was no ordinary dream. Tracey explains this in her moving story.

Vivid and peaceful

I've had two dreams in which I believe I've had a visit from my grandma who passed away about fourteen years ago. I usually have quite muddled dreams that dot around all over the place – but twice

I've dreamt about my nan and these dreams have been really vivid but peaceful. We've basically just sat holding hands and not saying anything and I can remember feeling the touch of her skin. When I've woken up I've felt really comforted and happy.

I'm a 49-year-old senior nurse and met my soul mate, Luke, twenty-five years ago. I was engaged (unhappily) at the time we met. The first time I saw him I knew on the spot that he would be the father of my children. Within two weeks we were together and twenty-five years later are married with three children.

At the end of June my husband was putting the hose away and tripped over his beloved dog and after the fall a large lump appeared on his neck. Two days later we were told that he had advanced lung cancer that they would not be able to cure. He went through three months of chemo with no side effects, intensive radiotherapy, again with no side effects, and up until six days before he died no one would have known that he was even unwell. His death was not expected at this stage and the day before we had been told that he had about two years.

I'm adopted and decided to get away for a few weeks after his death and stay with my birth mother. My daughter gave birth to our first grandchild three weeks after Luke died and I had not been able to feel any emotion for the child, although I hid this as best I could. I went to stay with my birth mother in Kent as she is very like me in the way she thinks and can read my feelings without speaking. The first night there I slept my first full night's sleep since Luke's death, which was strange in itself as I had only ever been to her house once in the past, many years ago. While I slept I had a crystal-clear dream that I can still see in my mind. Luke was sitting opposite me at a large wooden pub table. He looked fit and tanned and wore a red T-shirt and had his sunglasses on top of his head. The dream was so clear when I woke up that I actually forgot for a second that he had died. I felt comforted by the dream and some of my sorrow went.

When I checked my mobile my daughter who had just given birth had sent me a text. She told me that last night she had also had an amazingly clear and vivid dream. She said she was sitting at a large wooden table opposite me in the sunshine. She said a napkin kept flicking her in the face and although she couldn't see him she said she just knew it was Daddy as he likes to take the mickey. My daughter does not really believe in the psychic world but I'm sure this has given her something to think about.

My sister had given me your book the day I arrived in Kent, saying that she had been sent the book for Christmas. She had read it and decided that she was meant to give it to me to read. Imagine my surprise when I read the section on visitation dreams in your book! You have no idea how much comfort this gave me. I have now finished the book and ordered everything you have written. It has unlocked my own ability, which I always knew I had but have always been a bit frightened of.

In addition to night visions Tracey believes she has also had other reassuring signs from the other side.

I have to date had dozens of angel/Luke things that I have now recorded and when I feel very low I read them back to help and remind me. My youngest child is twelve and was very close to her father. She has always been very open about her psychic feelings and talks to her daddy often and tells me what he has said. Much of what she has said she couldn't have known before as they were special things that only Luke and I knew.

The one thing I am sure about is that two days after his death his spirit came home. My friend was here. It was around midnight and we both heard a key in the lock and the front door open. Luke's dog, who he loved to bits, went mad and charged out into the hall. We could hear his claws scrabbling as they do when he is being petted on the wooden floor. My friend said it must be her 17-year-old son who had changed his mind and come back from his friends early. With that the dog came into the room and was wagging his whole body as he only did for Luke. We both felt a little strange and went out to investigate as we had not heard the door shut, just open. The door was shut and locked and no one was in the house. I had an overpowering sense that my friend should leave, that Luke needed me to be alone. While I was in the bath the dog started to bark madly on Luke's side of the bed. When I got into bed, instead of being cold the bed felt warm. I am sure that it was Luke's spirit returning to me.

Like Tracey, both Lorna and Nia believe they have received signs of comfort and hope from beyond. Let's begin with Lorna's tale.

Utter shock

My ex came back to say goodbye one night just as I was about to go to sleep. I felt his presence sit on the bed beside me and take hold of my hands. He gave me comfort and apologised for what he had put me through. He had always been a very dominant character and this still came through, but he told me he was in utter shock that he had passed over as he totally didn't believe that he would die; he was only forty-seven years old. He also didn't believe in spirits or angels or in an afterlife and had got a tremendous shock on his passing! He said he hadn't understood my belief in angels (I have always been sensitive to the world of spirit, from a young child) but he knew now that I had been right.

Let's follow on with Nia's story.

The other side

I have just finished reading *An Angel Changed My Life*, which I really enjoyed. It says at the back to write in if we have an experience or insight to share.

Well, my story begins when my mother died in April 1990. A few months after she had died I was in bed. By my bed I had a little wooden stool that I had made for Mum in school and I had things on it, like scrapbooks and magazines. I thought I was having a dream: I heard someone telling me to move the scrapbooks because they wanted to sit, but I didn't know who it was. Anyway, when I woke up the next morning the stool had moved to the other side of my bedroom and there was nothing on it. I didn't remember moving the things until I saw them on the other side of the room.

When I mentioned this to my sister, Linda, she said exactly the same thing had happened to her on the same night it happened to me.

She had also heard someone telling her that they wanted to sit down. I still think about that to this day, nearly twenty-one years later. Did my mum speak to me that night?

And sometimes those who have passed away try to reach out to us through modern technology. This next story wasn't sent to me but I read about it online.

We love you

On the evening of 12 September 2008 a Los Angeles Metrolink train crashed. Among the dead was a man called Chuck Peck. His family, knowing that Chuck was on the train, kept getting calls from his cellphone. No voice was on the other end of the line and all that could be heard was static.

All night long, Chuck's sons, brother, stepmother, sister and fiancée got the phone calls from his phone. Chuck's son believed his dad was alive and trying to contact them and so he kept yelling into the phone: 'We love you, hang in there. They are coming to get you.'

At 3.28 a.m. the series of phone calls stopped and one hour later the body of Chuck was recovered by firefighters at the scene. Coroner's officials told Chuck's family members that he was killed instantly. His body showed no sign that he lived for even a short time after the crash.

Phone calls from the departed appear in this story from Christine.

Peaceful silence

Having read you book *An Angel Spoke to Me* I am 100 per cent sure my parents tried to reassure me from the afterlife that they were fine.

I will tell you what I mean. Twenty years ago my mum died in March. The night of the funeral I had a phone call. There was no one on the other end, just silence. I had this overwhelming feeling it was my mum and to this day I still believe it was her trying to reassure me that she was fine; even though there was no sound on the phone, it made me feel so peaceful. The same thing happened when my dad died, sixteen years ago, in April. The night of the funeral the phone went again, and there was no sound, just silence. I knew it was my dad. It was his way of telling me he was fine. I do still miss my mum and dad but I know they are at peace.

I do believe there are angels and higher beings around us. I have often felt somebody close by and my grandfather, who died forty years ago, just pops into my head. Another time I sensed my aunt. I smelt her perfume. It is lovely to think that those who have passed over are all around us, looking out for us even if we can't see them.

It may surprise you to know that communication with the world of spirit via electrical devices has been a matter of interest for a number of scientists, inventors and thinkers over the last century. Perhaps the most famous of these great minds was the inventor Thomas Edison who was born into a family of spiritualists and was fascinated by the idea of the mind surviving into the afterlife. Edison believed it might be possible for him to develop a telephone or electrical device that would enable communication with the dead and in a 1920 interview with *Scientific American* he is on record as stating that such a device might give spirits a better chance of reaching out to the living. Sadly, Edison died before he could complete his work on the device, but what an intriguing possibility.

Phone calls from the dead, like full-blown angel sightings, are rare, but a number have been well documented over the years and on occasion I do get sent stories and emails on the subject, proving that as far as modern technology is concerned angels aren't shy and they can use telephones or mobiles as well as computers and TV screens to communicate. Typically this happens when people ask for a sign and then the telephone rings and there is no one there and when they use 'ring back' the caller is unidentified or the number does not exist. It is rarer to hear a voice at the end of the telephone line but that is exactly what happened to Camilla, as she explains.

Hello

When I was about nine, my grandma was still alive. The last few years of her life must have been terrible for her as she suffered from Alzheimer's. I remember my parents taking me to see her in the nursing home where she lived and she just seemed to be wasting away. I was really scared to see someone so frail but my parents wanted to visit her before she died.

A week after this I was sitting in the kitchen doing my homework when Mum's mobile phone rang. I called Mum to answer it but she was busy upstairs and asked me to. I rummaged through her bag and took the call. It was Grandma.

'Hello. It's Grandma here. Don't worry. Everything will be all right. Tell your parents. Don't worry. Everything's going to be fine.'

So I hung up and told my mum what Grandma has said but she didn't believe me because Grandma was too ill to be using phones.

An hour later we received a call from my great-aunt. She told us that my grandma had died about an hour ago. This freaked me out as this was exactly the time I had received my phone call. I didn't remind my mum about the phone call I had taken as I knew they wouldn't believe me. It's a secret that I've kept with me all this time and it is such a relief to finally share it now with other believers.

Stories like Camilla's featuring phone calls from the dead have even become a subject of university research in their own right. Cal Cooper, a psychologist from Sheffield University, is currently conducting an impressive new research project on the subject and his research papers cite numerous cases that defy logical explanation. If you'd like to find out more about his work you can check out his website or contact him on: www.calcooper.com

Carol didn't receive a phone call but a text.

Together again

My mother, who was ninety, passed away in a care home in October 2010. My husband, sister, niece and I were at her bedside. Mum had been ill for some time but it was still very sad to lose her as

I didn't feel we were over losing Dad in 2004 yet. I was at the funeral directors making arrangements for Mum's funeral when I had a new text message from my sister, followed by an old text she had sent me several weeks before which concerned Mum. This has happened several times since – a new text followed by an old text that mentions Mum or Dad. I would like to think that Mum and Dad are trying to tell us they are watching over us and are together again.

I've made it clear in this book that there are countless ways for angels to touch our lives and our hearts, and one of these ways is through the spirits of those we have loved and lost. Sometimes this can happen in the seemingly most everyday way – but to the person involved it is deeply special. For Chelsea the simple gift of a necklace brought comfort and hope.

The necklace

Firstly, I want to thank you for your very inspiring book *An Angel Changed My Life*. This book has made me think so much about my life and I've been reading it slowly so I don't have to finish it.

I have never been religious, but I've always been curious about angels. It began when I was thirteen and a boy I liked called me an angel and it took my breath away; the love and warmth I felt from those words. Sounds silly, I know, but then a year later my beautiful grandma passed away due to cancer, leaving my entire family devastated. We are a close family and my mum, aunties and cousins were all heartbroken.

Come Christmas we all gathered to celebrate, as we did every year. We decided to invite one of Grandma's friends who I had briefly met once. During lunch she pulled me aside to give me something. She told me Grandma would have wanted me to have this; it was a small blue sapphire angel on a necklace. She hardly said anything else and walked off. I was shocked and curious as to why none of my cousins got anything.

I believe that necklace was sent to me by Grandma, to give me reassurance and possibly as I'm the oldest granddaughter to give me the strength to look after everyone. My mum and I often stare into the night sky and we know she's out there somewhere. Seven years later and I'm still wearing that necklace and it still gives me great comfort.

Familiar scents associated with a departed loved one can also bring feelings of comfort and hope, as can flowers that survive way past their expiration date. Olivia's story illustrates . . .

A sign?

I'm not sure whether I'm reading too much into this but I would like to think that I'm not. My grandma died last year from a stroke. I was really close to her and we were all with her when she died. It was the saddest time of my life but I have never felt like she has gone. I often think I need to go and see her then I remember I can't.

For the day of the funeral we had a wreath made out of lily of the valley – her favourite flower. When we were putting this down onto the grave a small stem came off and was by my feet. I picked it

187

up and took it home. I put it in a glass by the window and it lasted nearly three months there! I couldn't believe it as I had other flowers that had flower food and so on and none lasted longer than a week or so. I like to think it's a sign she was still here with us.

Sue explains how a bird sighting eased her grief after the death of her father. Here is her story.

Big surprises

Why I bought your book *An Angel Spoke to Me* is a big surprise to me as I have never really thought about angels. I suppose a lot of people just think it's like fairies, something made up to comfort little children. But after reading through a few pages I began to see that things have happened to me that I just never thought about hard enough, or just ignored.

I was never very close to my father when I was a child. I was a difficult child, wild, and fought all discipline, but as I grew older and had my own family he was always there for me. I think as I was growing up my father was just strict and I rebelled against his rules. As I grew and had my own family I understood what he had tried to do.

Well, what my story is about is that my dad was ill for the last two years of his life and lived some 200 miles away and I did not get to see him very much (this I have always felt guilty about). I used to speak to him on the phone maybe once a week. I often spoke to my sister about him and although I was in my late forties she still seemed able to make me do what she wanted (maybe this was because we were brought up in children's homes from the age of about six and she was my only real friend through those years). On this particular occasion she told me that I was not to ring him for at least two weeks as he (she said) was being stubborn and not doing what he should. I did as she told me to do and my dad died without me seeing or speaking to him for those two weeks. I had thought that he would always be here, so I blamed myself for him dying on his own and me not talking to him. I was in a state and found everyday living a task that I had to get through each day. I missed him so much and the pain was as raw as a knife cutting into me, but in time I began to adjust. It's true what people say, that the pain gets less raw and you begin to live again, even though you always think of your loved one.

One morning about a year after Dad died I found white feathers around the house, one in my front room and another in my bedroom. I had read somewhere that this could be a sign from a loved one and honestly thought, That's not Dad (not sure why I even thought of him at that time) because he never believed in all that. But as I sat down in my living room a pigeon flew in, it flew around the room and back out. I was amazed – it didn't fly into anything, nor did it not know the way out. It was as though someone or something knew exactly what it was doing.

It has not happened since and after that day I felt Dad had come back to say he was now free of his disability and was happy, and I was not to keep blaming myself for something that was of no importance to him now. Maybe you think this email is a bit mixed up but I have written it as it came into my head and know that my dad understands it, so maybe that is the most important thing in all this.

For Denise, whose story follows on below, something once again unusual and deeply personal to her has reassured her that her mother in spirit is never far away.

Fly away

I find your books very interesting, especially about angels appearing as animals. My mother died in January 2010 and my sister and I nursed her in the last few weeks of her life. During this time she kept asking us to make sure her robin was fed – she always had a robin that came down daily for the food she put out – so we always did this to reassure her.

I have always encouraged the birds in my garden, but never seemed to get robins until this year. Now I see a robin almost daily – I am sure they are nesting close by and believe it is a sign that my mother has come down to say hello. I also find that as soon as I have a problem, this robin flies down into the garden and again I think that it's Mum's way of telling me all will be well. It's quite a comfort to me.

Denise sent me this further email as a follow-up.

I emailed you about two months ago to tell you about the robin in my garden that appeared after my mother's death. Well, since then I have had another most unusual experience.

It started seven years ago when I decided to contact all my long-lost cousins. We all lived down the same street in London as children and played together, but once grown up and married we all moved further afield and lost touch. Then after forty years I contacted all of them. My cousin David replied the quickest with a lovely letter and phone call, and needless to say I told him we would visit ASAP. We all got on really well and our regular visits were full of laughter from morning till night. Very sadly, my lovely cousin was taken from us suddenly with cancer. We had grown so close and it was a great shock to all of us – he was only sixty-five. One day after he had died I looked out of my window and there were two robins together – most unusual as robins are territorial in the garden and usually fight. My mother was my cousin's godmother so I felt that they were letting me know that they were both with me; it was a great comfort at this very sad time.

Sophie wrote to me to ask me if I thought her father in spirit spoke to her in a simple but profound way and I wrote back to tell her that her father had indeed found a way to communicate his eternal love for her.

Brief encounter

I recently lost my dad – two months ago today. It's his fiftieth birthday tomorrow and in the last few weeks things haven't really been going well for me at all. I've felt very low indeed, but I'm writing to you to share this experience I had as I held a picture of him in front of me and started talking to him. I told him that I felt as if I'd let him down and that he wouldn't be proud of me and at the same moment I was sitting there crying I saw a card he and his wife had got me when I'd passed my exams saying how proud he was of me and everything. The incredible thing is that at the bottom it says he will always be proud of me no matter what. These words come at a time when I really needed them. Do you think that I had a brief angel encounter?

In the next chapter you'll see that angel calling cards or signs are often the same as those used by spirits of the departed to reach out to us because, to risk repeating myself, all messages of hope and comfort from the other side are angel-inspired. This chapter would swell to fill an entire book if I tried to mention all the different ways loved ones in spirit can talk to us. I'm just giving you a taster here to open your mind and heart to the idea that loved ones in spirit are closer than you think and can communicate their love and reassurance in countless different ways. Sometimes this communication may take the form of a vision, a feeling or a vivid dream, but more often than not it will manifest in everyday ways that to the person involved are deeply reassuring and comforting.

I'm sure rational explanations could be found for all the stories so far, but in each case I'm sure you will agree that if you keep an open mind, which I hope you always will, it is impossible to dismiss the equally real possibility that they could also be communications from beyond the grave.

Alive in death

Many of us fear death and find it hard to think about our own deaths or the deaths of loved ones, but after the many years

I have been reading stories from people who have caught glimpses of the beyond I am utterly convinced that death is just another natural phase in our existence. It is not an end but a wonderful new beginning. As the ancient Celts would say, it is the Land of the Young.

The first time someone told me that you start dying the moment you are born I found it really depressing, but with my new understanding I have now come to realise that dying is a natural part of living, I regard it as a wonderful thing because it brings you closer to heaven. Every time you fall asleep and dream, or view the world with angel eyes, a part of your consciousness 'dies', leaves your body and travels to the land of spirit.

It seems right to put Helen's story here.

The painting

I loved my granny, so when she died I was devastated. I just sobbed my heart out, the pain was unbearable. One day I sat below the painting of her above my fire, looked at it and said, 'Oh, Granny,' and felt deep pain as I cried. Suddenly it was as if I was enclosed inside a bubble, and with that came the most wonderful feeling of love, peace and, most of all, knowledge. I realised then that it was not my granny that was dead but me, and that this life was not real because real life and truth were over there. Since that day I have never cried when someone died, and if I do shed a tear it is not for them but for me as they have left me here.

The feeling inside that bubble will stay with me for the rest of my life. There is no way to explain how it felt.

Louise sent me this touching story about her mother.

My friend

My mother died at the age of ninety-three in March this year, and since then I've been drawn to reading books about angels. I've got all your books and I find them very comforting. I wonder what you make of this:

For the last eighteen months of her life my mother was very frail and had the beginnings of dementia, so with many misgivings the family found her a ground-floor room in a very loving care home in Norfolk. She settled well and enjoyed watching the birds on the bird table outside her window, but she said she missed us and had nothing to do. So when she told me that a friend often came to visit and the staff told me that this friend was imaginary I felt even worse. I believed that she had made up an imaginary friend because she was so lonely. When I telephoned her she often said the friend was in the room with her and one time I suggested I might speak to her on the phone but my mother said she'd disappeared into her bathroom. My mother had only one week's illness, during which she gradually faded away and kept assuring us that she was comfortable, that nothing hurt and at one point after a brief nap said, 'It's so beautiful.'

Now she's gone I'm wondering whether she had a glimpse of the world to come in her dream. And even more I'm now wondering if the imaginary friend was really an angel who had come to keep her company. My mother always liked angels but she was not fanciful in any way.

And just as dying is a natural part of living, so is living a natural part of dying. Nothing proves this more than reports of near-death experiences when a person's life hangs in the balance or reports of those who have stepped into the afterlife and never felt as alive as during their experience. All fear of death seems to vanish once a person has caught a glimpse of the beyond.

John sent me this exceptional account.

Extraordinary vision

My name is John and I am seventy-two years old. Both myself and my lovely wife Carol believe in angels. I'm just an ordinary man who has been gifted with an extraordinary vision and I know for certain that life continues forever. Please be so kind as to read this account of an experience I had in 1976 when my beloved first wife Deanna passed away.

Deanna had been ill for two years, a time not only of suffering, pain and sadness, but also of much happiness. On Saturday 12 June 1976, my beloved wife passed peacefully away in the hospital at Bournemouth. I clearly remember my knowing that now she was all right, that her sufferings were over and that she was at peace.

I presently returned home and at about 10.30 p.m. retired to bed, being now, for the first time that day, quite on my own. I switched on the bedside lamp; I switched off the main bedroom light and got into bed, meaning to reflect on all that had happened.

As I lay back in bed my head had no sooner touched the pillow than I began to feel a great peacefulness and calmness envelop me. Suddenly I saw, as if from afar, several golden-coloured specks of light which were travelling towards me. These lights were followed by more and still more, until my field of vision was filled by them. As they got nearer to me they grew larger and became beautiful golden orbs of light which shimmered.

The orbs, as they approached me, changed into circles of brilliant shimmering light and they then seemed to splash literally against my eyes as they reached them. I remember feeling astonished at what was taking place, but this feeling changed to one of acceptance of the phenomenon as I became more and more absorbed with what followed. There was by now a multitude of the lights, which then merged or changed into a golden aura.

Suddenly, within this background of light, I saw a single grey shape appear and just as quickly vanish. Then another similar shape appeared and went, and then there were four and then thirty of these shapes coming and going before my eyes. They were all grey and quite featureless but had outlines very similar to, say, a potato! They were basically oval but with small, well-rounded nodules. Also the shapes were all vibrating against the now still background at an enormous rate. The strange thing was that although there were no distinguishing features I just knew that I was looking at the souls of my family that had gone before me – my grandparents, uncles, aunts and so on – and I became aware of a great sense of love enveloping me.

More and more of these shapes were both appearing and vanishing, until presently there were vast numbers of them, thronging from right before my eyes and then becoming smaller as they receded from me into a great arc which disappeared into the golden light. It was literally as though I was looking on part of the very host of heaven itself . . .

While I was watching all this I told myself that if I turned off the bedside lamp then all of this would go away because it was just a dream and I was kidding myself! So I reached my arm over and switched off the light.

Well! Far from the vision disappearing, I now found, with the room in virtually total darkness, that I was looking at the unfolding panorama with an even greater contrast between colours and the background . . .

The next thing that happened was that I felt as though I was being lifted off my back and turned over to lie on my side. Then I fell asleep almost immediately and did not wake till the next morning.

During the next morning I received a visit from the surgeon who had fought hard for Deanna and whom I had come to regard as a trusted friend. It was good of him to call and, as we sat in the lounge I told him about the wonderful vision I had had of the life to come. I could think of no other way to describe it. When I had finished I asked him what he thought about it all. I could see he was visibly moved as he, a man of great faith and a lay preacher, said, 'Well, sometimes the bereaved are given to see things.'

Ever since this extraordinary vision – which really almost seemed quite thrust upon me – I have known from within that there is a life to come and that this world we live in is not our real home and that whilst death is the end for the physical part of us, our souls are destined to return from whence they came – through the Gateway and into the life eternal that has been prepared for us.

197

I believe too that what I saw was not only meant to help me through the ensuing sadness and difficulties that the bereaved have to bear, but it was also meant to point the way ahead and remind me that we are meant to live our lives to the full, doing the best we can according to our circumstances, and that we should try to help others too – knowing that not only are each of us responsible for our destiny, and that we reap what we sow, but also that none of us is ever truly alone as we journey though this strange and beautiful life.

Above all else, I still remember clearly from all those years ago that as my eyes beheld the silent and majestically beautiful panorama, I felt myself being enveloped in an overwhelming presence of love – which came unannounced – when I most needed it. That feeling has stayed with me ever since.

This isn't the full account of what John sent me but I hope I've included enough to give you a very real sense of his extraordinary vision. Especially profound, I feel, is what John says towards the end of his account. Many people who have caught a glimpse of the afterlife tell me that not only do they lose all fear of death, they also fall in love with their lives again. They live with a renewed sense of purpose, meaning and joy, and make every minute count, but you don't need to see angels or have a brush with death to do that. You can start living life as it was meant to be lived – to the full – right here, right now.

In the next chapter of this book you'll find plenty of stories of people living their lives in spirit in the way they were meant to be lived, but before that, I couldn't think of a better way to end a chapter entitled 'The Land of the Young' than with this astonishing story sent to me by Mandy. I'm placing it here because I believe it unites the themes discussed in this chapter in a beautiful way and shows that when life is lived in spirit there really is no death, no ageing and no fear.

Woken up

It would be about eighteen years ago now that I passed out because of a really bad stomach ache. This was something that had happened before and has happened since, but on this occasion I managed to call out to my husband just before, knowing that I was going to pass out. What happened next is something that my husband has told me.

He came into the bathroom and I'd apparently fallen and swallowed my tongue. I was on the floor, making a gurgling sound. He said he'd never felt so frightened as my face looked like a 'death face'. He had to put his fingers in my mouth to pull my tongue out of the back of my throat. All I remember of the incident, something that still stays with me today, is the indescribable feeling of annoyance at having been woken up from the most wonderful dream. I remember the wonderful sound of children's laughter and immense love.

It's hard to put into words the annoyance I felt at being 'brought back'. If you imagine the most wonderful dream you've ever had, multiply it by ten, and then get woken up and multiply the feeling of annoyance by fifty, this is probably close to the feeling I had. It was late in the evening that this happened, so it definitely wasn't the sound of children outside that I heard. I didn't see anything, just had the wonderful feeling of love and heard the joyous and beautiful sound of children's laughter.

Do you think I had some kind of out-of-body experience and felt 'something' of the spirit side? If this is the feeling you get when you cross over then I'm in no way frightened when it's my time. The feeling was absolutely blissful, absolutely wonderful.

CHAPTER SIX

Celtic Hearts

Always remember to forget the troubles that passed away.
But never forget to remember the blessings that come each day.

Irish blessing for the journey

Remember, in Gaelic there isn't a word for 'hello' – other people are greeted with an acknowledgement of the divine presence within and around them.

I hope that reading this book will have helped you become more open to the very real possibility that something wonderful and magic is alive within and around you, even though you may not be able to see, hear, feel or touch it. The real question you should be asking yourself is: are you ready to open yourself to this magic? Even when life isn't going your way or darkness falls, can you reach deep within and be open to the incredible idea that angels are watching over you? If you truly want to, you can find those angels and experience the magic, joy, wonder and hope they bring to your life and to everyone and everything you encounter, however mundane or ordinary.

The more you open your heart to the angels within and around you, the greater the possibility of recognising their presence. While it is true that the ability to see magic in the ordinary is ingrained in the Irish, the next selection of stories in this book were sent to me by people who again were not Irish, but who discovered they had the ability to see both themselves and the world around them through angel eyes. In other words, they found or rediscovered their Celtic hearts.

Angels at work

One of the most awe-inspiring things about the work I do as an angel author is discovering just how many people from all over the world interact with angels on a daily basis. Some of these people believe they can actually see or hear angels, others have not had full-blown encounters but have found that something extraordinary, unexpected and unexplainable in their daily lives has opened them up to the invisible world all around and within them.

When we encounter the extraordinary in our daily lives, we can either choose to explain it away as coincidence, chance or luck, or we can regard it as something deeply meaningful and angel-inspired. Since every one of us is in control of what we believe in our hearts, why not choose a viewpoint that opens doors to the possibility of joy and hope instead of one that closes out those options? Why not trust in the philosophy that things happen for a reason? Why not believe in miracles and that things are not always what they appear to be? Why not believe in angels?

In the next round of stories, meaningful coincidences occurred in the course of everyday lives, and for the people directly involved there is no doubt in their minds that angels were at work. Their experiences could easily be explained away as luck or chance by sceptics, but when someone finds themselves in the centre of a series of meaningful experiences they are often filled with a sense of awe, hope and wonder that can completely turn their lives around. They are absolutely convinced that the world is a magical place where angels are at work, and far from contradicting this opinion, modern physics, which seems to suggest that nothing is ever random, may even back it up.

So you see, there is more to everyday life than meets the eye, and sometimes all we need to do is open our minds and allow our angels to do their work. A closed mind is a natural predator of angels, so the next time you find yourself explaining something special that has happened in your life as a stroke of luck or chance, I urge you to at the very least consider the possibility that your guardian angel may have been at work. The chance meeting, the life-saving encounter, a lost object found or a flash of insight at just the right moment may all be signs of an unseen power. Sometimes even the most mundane of events, or ones that are easy to explain away rationally, can be ascribed to angels.

I promise you that as soon as you start to open yourself to the idea of angels in this way, nothing in your life will ever feel the same again. You will feel a burst of energy, hope, joy and fulfilment that you may not have known before; all signs that there are beings of light all around you, and most important of all, that an aspiring angel is spreading its wings within you.

Let's start with this story, sent to me by Nigel.

Out of the blue

Out of the blue I was attracted to your book in a shop and then purchased the digital version for my Kindle. I found it totally absorbing as I have found myself on a spiritual journey after watching *The Big Silence* on the BBC – before that I was a spiritual wasteland. My mother died nearly two years ago and this did have a big impact on me, so perhaps I was secretly looking for something.

My angel story is regarding my mother's funeral. I was very close to my mother; my father was disabled at home for many years and died when I was eighteen. During the last three years of her life she was slowly lost to us through dementia, which was hard to bear. She eventually lost the battle but I was able to spend the last day with her. The funeral was a week later.

We live over two hours away so on the day we set off early to make sure we would be on time; but the traffic that day was unusually terrible. Eventually it looked like we might not make it, so I phoned and said we would go straight to the crematorium. We were forced to leave the motorway and continue across country. Approaching my home town I realised we would pass the undertakers and, totally unplanned, the hearse literally pulled out right in front of us! We then followed it all the way.

At the time I thought it was just a coincidence but since reading your book I now view it differently.

Chris got in touch with me to tell me about a stunning coinci-dence that she believes led her to her soul mate.

Left behind

One summer's night when I was nine years old I went to a local pub with my parents. I took my bike with me and we sat in the garden of the pub. My parents got chatting to another couple who had their 10-year-old son with them. When it was time to go, we all walked home together. We had gone a short way down the road when I realised I had left my bike behind, so the boy ran back with me to get it. We never spoke to each other on the way and we never saw the family again.

Some years later when I was in my teens I was at a roller-skating rink and sat down to put my boots on. The laces to one of the boots snapped and I cursed. The boy sitting next to me, who was also putting his boots on, looked up and gave me the most wonderful smile I had ever seen. It lit his face up and I was instantly attracted to him. Needless to say, we started dating and when he told his parents about me his mum said she thought I must be the girl they had met all that time ago as I lived in the same area . . .

Yes, it was me, and we have been happily married for the past forty-two years. I think the angels definitely had something to do with that, don't you?

Coincidences play a huge part in bringing people together into a meaningful relationship. In fact, when you think about the billions of people on the planet, isn't it a miracle that any of us find our soul mate?

In addition to meaningful coincidences, another astonishing way that angels can reveal themselves to us is through our heart-felt prayers. This next story, sent to me by Mary, shows how the power of prayer can help give us strength during painful times in our lives.

Time to sleep now

I have just read your book and I feel like I was meant to read it. I also feel that I need to write to you to tell you about an experience I had when I had to put my beloved dog to sleep last July. She was eighteen and used to fall over, but always barked for me to pick her up. I used to have to put her to toilet in the early hours. I didn't realise for a long time how tired all this was making me, but eventually I knew I had to make a decision for the both of us. My husband died in April 2000 and my youngest daughter in 2001, so I have had my fair share of sorrow. I think that is why I hung on to my dog for so long, but her life really was not so good in the end and we both needed peace.

I got down on my knees and prayed for strength to deal with the situation. I have never told anyone about this as I do not usually share my feelings, but as I prayed I felt the strength come through the top of my head and then spread to my whole body. I was able finally to call the vet and request for it to be done. When I stepped outside to get some air there was a feather there. I know I made the right decision for both of us, and that we are both now at peace.

Although the presence of angels is often reported during times of crisis, because our minds and hearts are more open then, don't fall into the trap of thinking that dramatic situations are always the catalyst. As Emma's story shows, sometimes beings of light can reveal themselves in seemingly insignificant events.

Small miracles

My angel experiences so far have not been dramatic but I wanted to share them with you, firstly because one happened today. I have just returned to work from maternity leave and am desperately unhappy to be leaving my little girl. Today was her first day at nursery and when I dropped her off, she cried, which was so upsetting. I drove to work in tears and straight away prayed to the angels to help her be happy without me and asked them to please, please take care of her. I must have been talking to them for five or ten minutes. When I got to work, I called the nursery and they said Holly was fine and had stopped crying after about five minutes. I believe she may have been comforted by angels – what do you think? As a mother, I want to protect her all the time but knowing that angels are around her gives me great comfort.

My other experience is more light-hearted and may make you smile. I think these angels have a sense of humour – or maybe I just ask for little favours (I am convinced there are car parking angels). I was in the supermarket and wanted some milk from a high shelf that I just couldn't reach. There was hardly anyone around and no assistants. I thought to myself: If only someone tall could come round the corner and help me . . . Lo and behold, about three seconds later, a man of over six foot appeared and happily reached my milk for me. A very small miracle compared with some other inspiring stories I've been reading, but proof to me that our angels may even influence the seemingly insignificant encounters in our lives.

It is my firm belief that every one of us has had signs or messages from our guardian angels at some time or other, but we just don't realise or recognise them for what they are at the time. A good example is when you are forced to take a different route to work and find our later that you avoided an accident, or at the last minute you decide to go to a party and meet your soul mate or someone who has a positive influence on your life. Flashes of insight or an overwhelming desire to give and not expect anything in return, especially when a strong desire seems to come from out of the blue, are all examples of your guardian angel at work, as are overwhelming feelings of gratitude, love, joy and peace or sudden strokes of good fortune. In addition to such happy 'coincidences', other commonly reported angel calling cards include sensing changes in the atmosphere, perhaps warmth or a tingling sensation down your spine. You might smell a fragrant, sweet aroma with no likely source, or develop an unexplained sweet taste in your mouth. Also common is feeling an angelic breeze when there is no door or window open, or the brush of angel wings gently caressing or kissing you. It's such a gentle loving touch, like that of a loving parent, and it is just to let you know that your angels are there and that they care for you. Seeing coloured lights out of nowhere, or brilliant light in and around you, even with your eyes closed, is another sign. And if you feel a flutter in your tummy this might just be your guardian angel talking to you through your gut instinct or intuition. Whenever any of these sensations happen to you – and they will – use them as opportunities to relax, count your blessings and thank your guardian angel for walking beside you.

And then there are perhaps the most common – common only in the sense that they are reported most often – signs of angels at work in your life: clouds, flowers, rainbows, words in a book and lyrics in a song, coins that turn up in unusual places, lost items found, butterflies and white feathers. The next batch of stories feature many of these well-known angel calling cards, beginning with perhaps the most well-known of them all: white feathers.

I love this email, sent to me by Anne.

A bright cloud

Apart from the loss of my mum I would say life had been good to me, but life changed dramatically and devastatingly within the last two years and it's been hard: with marriage break-up, family torn apart, and the sudden death of my beloved brother, a really dark cloud hung over me.

Recently I had occasion to visit the town where we used to live, and I took a walk through a store; just passing time, I spotted your book *An Angel Healed Me* and had to buy it. I could not put it down and felt comforted even just reading it. I can feel my energies rise, family rifts are healing, problems are literally disappearing.

I finished reading the book yesterday. I followed your advice and called my angels, spoke to them, asked them for a sign that they were with me – I asked for a white feather or something just to convince me or maybe clarify my optimism for the future.

Today I visited my father and before I left he handed me a bag which contained a box of six eggs from his hens. Tonight for my supper I decided to have a fresh boiled egg. I opened the box and there on the inside of the lid was a beautiful white feather, obviously from the hens, but I think I got my white feather!

This next story, sent to me by Emma's sister, also talks about the spiritual comfort that the sudden and unexpected appearance of a white feather can bring.

Be strong

After reading two of your books I have become inspired and also open to the spiritual world around me, and now receive many signs of an angel being present. My sister Emma died when I was four; up until then she was the one who I loved more than anyone, and because her death was not long after my birthday I blamed myself although she died from natural causes (diabetes).

Anyway, when I am alone and upset I will sit in my room and cry, but will soon be cheered up by a scent – it is Emma's scent as she is letting me know she is still there for me. She often plays tricks like popping every bulb in her family's home on the same night; some people may say it's all coincidence but I don't think it is, I believe it's my beloved Emma letting everyone know she's still here and we shouldn't forget that. The other night I was reading your book and got to the white feather stories, which truly inspired me, so that night I asked for a sign from Emma, hoping I would receive a feather, but to my disappointment I didn't get one. Upset, I decided the next day to go to her grave and, after I had poured my heart out, this white feather drifted in between me and the headstone. You could say it was chance, but I believe it's Emma telling me to be strong and that I will get through it.

Carol sent me this letter.

Chosen

Just after my dad passed away in 2004 I had an interview for a new job. I was walking down the road to my appointment when a white feather appeared beside me at shoulder level. It stayed with me next to my shoulder all the way to the door for my interview. I was nervous going for the job but felt more confident after seeing the feather and would like to think it helped me to be chosen for the job, which I was!

Sometimes angels will reveal themselves to us through angel- or wing-shaped clouds – again appearing at just the right time. In Michelle's case it was a year since the death of her beloved nan. She kindly sent in a photograph of the cloud. I wish I could share it with you here but her words will have to do.

Picture perfect

Your book inspired me to forward you a copy of a picture that I took of what I believe to be a beautiful angel in the sky! I saw her when I was out on a family trip. All of my family was together. We had taken a ride in a steam train to an historic town. As the train pulled into the station, I glanced out of the window and said to my parents, 'Look at the beautiful angel in the sky.' She was huge, and we quickly took photos. Funnily enough we saw the angel exactly a year to the day that my nana passed.

When you look closely at the wings and stomach area there are love hearts interspaced throughout the angel's body. Whenever I am struggling with life, I look at my special angel picture and take great comfort in the love that is pouring from her body! Hope you love the picture as much as I do!

This story is from Dannii.

Growing closer

I believe in angels and feel like I am growing closer to them all the time. I know they love us no matter what.

The other day I was a bit anxious and went outside to look at the night sky. I saw the moon, which always gives me a great sense of hope and light, and the clouds seemed to form a smiley/happy face in the sky. Then a few minutes later the clouds turned into angel wings – which I thought was truly amazing too. It made me feel happy and reassured me that everything will be OK.

Lynn also believes angels sent her a message of love and hope from Cecily, her beloved daughter in spirit, in the night sky.

Plain as a pikestaff

What happened on Cecily's birthday was wonderful. I was sitting in the garden on the evening of her birthday and was wondering what Cecily would be doing now and generally going over the past twenty years . . . I looked up to the sky, which was completely black – no stars, no moon.

I said out loud, 'Cecily, please let me know if you are around,' and out of the darkness the moon appeared with two clouds next to it. One was in the shape of the letter C and the other in the shape of a heart . . . I know it sounds bonkers but it was as plain as a pikestaff!

In her story below, Toni talks about how she is finding her angels.

Look deep within

I hope you don't mind me getting in touch with you. I am currently reading your book *An Angel Spoke to Me* and am thoroughly enjoying it. It provides me with great comfort, particularly when I am reading it at bedtime. There are lots of stories within the book and references to angels that sound very similar to some experiences I have had myself, and if it's OK I wanted to share them with you to see what you think.

Just before Christmas 2010 I had a nervous breakdown. It was a couple of months later that I was in my local shopping centre with my boyfriend and I went into a bookshop, with no intention of buying a book, but then your book was there on the shelf, the last one, calling out to me to read it, so I knew I had to buy it.

Every time I pick up your book there is either a person's name or a story or message that is relevant to my situation at the time. For example, the mention of rainbows or the reference to butterflies, as I know someone whose mum passed away and a butterfly was present at his wedding as if his mum was there. The other day a butterfly flew right past my nose as I was at the cemetery visiting my nan and granddad with my mum.

Butterflies also feature in this story sent to me by Lisa.

On the edge

It was coming up to the second anniversary of my father-in-law's passing, and my husband decided to visit his mom to take some flowers to put on the shrine she had made in the garden. While he was having some time at this shrine I happened to call him and as we were talking he said a butterfly had landed on the memorial stone he had brought the previous Christmas for the shrine. We carried on talking and he commented again that the butterfly was still there. I told him to take a photo of it with his phone, which he did.

When he came home and showed me the photo there was the most beautiful butterfly perched on the edge of the memorial stone in front of some red flowers. A week later my friend who was visiting and has the gift of speaking to those in spirit turned and said to my husband, 'I have your dad here and he said he came to see you in the garden and he was by the red flowers.' My husband almost fell over but after the shock he was delighted. We explained to my friend what had happened and she was convinced my father-in-law was indeed the butterfly. My husband still keeps the photo of the butterfly on his phone and it gives him some comfort to think his much-loved dad is watching over him.

Scent and ethereal sounds feature in this next account sent to me by Gill.

Thank you for listening

I have not quite finished your book *An Angel Changed My Life* but felt I had to write to you. When I went into the library to choose new books to read I picked up your book off the 'Books others have read' shelf but put it back and then walked round the library and was drawn back to your book. I am loving reading it.

I may end up sending another email as I have had lots happen to me in my life, but wanted to share the time when I felt really low. Since my early twenties I had suffered quite a few miscarriages and then thanks to a fantastic Belgian gynaecologist I was offered an operation that meant I would be able to carry a child to full term. Just after my lovely son was born I was told that I would not be able to have any more children – at the time I was so grateful for my son that it didn't sink in and I just thought I'd have more (regardless of the danger). A year later I started bleeding heavily and felt a huge lump in my stomach. I visited a gynaecologist, this time in Germany (where we were living), and he gently told me I had a tumour and would have to have a hysterectomy. Until the tumour had been removed they would not be able to tell if it was malignant or not. We received the news two days before Christmas and were told to go home and enjoy our Christmas and that I would be admitted on 2 January.

We were both devastated – I was doubly so as at the back of my mind I still felt I would conceive more children. As my family were so far away I had to tell them over the phone and I spent over an hour sobbing with my sister. That night I had gone for a bath and was lying in the water worrying what might happen to my son if I had cancer. I started to think about my grandma, who had died the previous year, and looked up at the ceiling. I swear I saw the image of a lady who looked like my grandma holding babies in her arms, and then I smelt the really strong smell of cigarette smoke (my great-uncle, who I was also close to, smoked heavily). I just felt an overall feeling of calm and knew that whatever happened I would be all right.

Thankfully the tumour was caught in time and although it was just starting to display cancerous cells I required no further treatment. It made me reflect on life. Before the operation I had been very driven and so very organised – for example, every month when the bank statement came I would grill my husband about every last penny. After the operation I realised life was too short and I totally relaxed my outlook and took time out from my life to just chill and live each day to the full.

Since that day I have realised that spirits and angels are always around us. Whenever I feel low or tired the strong smell of cigarette smoke can be smelt – sometimes at night in my son's room or in my car (not one of us smokes). I think it is my great-uncle keeping an eye on our son and just letting me know that life will be fine.

A familiar fragrance also appears in this email, sent to me by Pam.

Follow me

I felt compelled to email you after finishing your inspiring book *An Angel Healed Me* – what a beautiful way for so many people to have been touched by angels. I strongly believe in angels and the spirit world; there is too much evidence to support the fact of their lovely existence. I myself have had angels help me when at my lowest ebb, and they have been with me at my highest. There really are too many incidents for me to mention, but I hope you don't mind me mentioning a few.

My lovely mum (-in-law), who loved me so much, and I loved her right back, went to heaven nineteen years ago. I nursed her, loved her, and was with her when the angels took her. About a year after her journey I walked into my hallway and the smell of her favourite perfume was so strong it made me very emotional to know that she had contacted me. Her spirit has also been present with my daughter on occasions when she has been troubled. Once, my daughter was driving home with her two children when her petrol gauge started flashing very low; she was very concerned as she was quite a distance from home, so she said out loud, 'Nan, please help me.' Two minutes afterwards a car pulled out in front of her and started driving very slowly. Then one of the children told her to look at the sign in the back of the car. It said 'Follow God'. This car went at a snail's pace then indicated left; my daughter followed, and there was a garage! She said, 'Thank you, Nan.'

This story from Sheila is about another well-reported angel calling card: something precious that was lost being found at a significant time.

Mystified

I would like to relate this incident to you because it is still such a mystery to me, even though it happened so long ago. In your book *An Angel Changed My Life* you have a chapter near the end relating to death and unusual experiences to do with life after death, which I do firmly believe in.

It was August 1984 and my husband was in Southampton General Hospital. He had a brain tumour and had consequently lost his power of speech and was not able to write. They both originate from the same area of the brain, it seems. I used to drive down to see him every day. A journey of eighty miles, it would take me at least one and a half to two hours each way because there were really bad road works and there was no way of avoiding them.

About a year before my husband became ill he had fitted special bolts on the wheel hubs of his Morris Minor. There had been a spate of tyre/wheel thefts in our area and he wanted to make sure it didn't happen to him, but it did mean you needed a special tool to get the wheels off.

My brother-in-law Tony said I must find out from John where he kept the tool for the wheel hubs in case I got a puncture with all the travelling I was doing. I asked John where the tool was and although I knew he understood what I wanted, he couldn't explain. I gave him a pen and paper to see if he could write it down but there was no response. I reasoned that the only place he would have kept this tool was in the car, so I decided to search for it. He had made a special tool-box under the back seat, so I had that out and searched the car in every nook and cranny I could reach, with no luck. Tony said he would look for it also, so he did the same and practically stripped the car looking for it. In the end he gave up looking and forced the bolts off with a hammer and chisel, and fitted ordinary locking bolts. As it happened, a week later I did get a puncture on the motorway and a kind taxi driver stopped and helped me.

The point of this story, though, is that I never thought any more about it, even though John did come home and regain a little of his speech and lived for another three months, for which I was so grateful.

Three days after John died I got the car out of the garage. My daughter was sitting in the car waiting for me and as I started to get into the car with her I saw something lying on the floor behind my seat. I leaned over to pick it up and knew immediately what it was. It was the special tool that I had been looking for all those months earlier. I asked my daughter if she knew how it had got on the floor behind her seat and she reacted like most teenagers would – she didn't really know what I was talking about. I simply do not know where that tool had come from. If it had been caught up underneath one of the seats why hadn't we found it earlier when we searched the car? And getting the car out of the garage had been a smooth operation so why had it suddenly become dislodged if it was stuck somewhere? Tony and I had searched that car with a fine-tooth comb. He was as mystified as I was when I told him and showed him. It was definitely the tool we had been searching for.

It was reading some of the stories about lost objects turning up at significant times in your book and that idea of angel calling cards brought this incident to mind. I am still as puzzled now as I was then. I believe that our loved ones stay with us as long as we need them.

Coins with significant dates on them turning up in unexpected places are another angel calling card, as are unexpected windfalls. This is what happened to Danuisa.

The powers above

As I work as a driving instructor, December was a really bad month for me this year. I could not work for ten days because of the snow, and, being Christmas, finances were very short and I was worried not just about paying my bills but about buying Christmas presents for my three sons. The bank refused to give me a temporary overdraft to see me into the New Year, therefore there was only one thing I could do – put a request out there to my guardian angels, then believe and leave it in their capable hands to help me through this tough period.

I was lucky enough to receive a loan from my eldest son to cover my bills over Christmas and the start of January, then lo and behold, the first week of January I received a telephone call, which at first I thought was someone winding me up. But it was not a joke. I had bought raffle tickets from a charity in December and had won second prize, £3000. I received the cheque in the post a week later. Again my guardian angels had come to my rescue and I was very grateful for their help. I was able to pay back my son immediately and get all my bills up to date.

I never cease to be amazed at the powers above.

Nia's story is also about coins.

Pennies from heaven?

I collect two-pound coins and put them in a savings tin that you have to have a can-opener to open. One night when I went to bed I happened to put my arm under my pillow and there was a two-pound coin there, which I thought was odd because I always put them straight in the tin and would never put them under my pillow. I even asked my boys if they knew anything about it, but even if they had found it there is no way they would have put it under my pillow; they would have kept it and spent it!

So where did it come from – was it pennies from heaven?

Angels are full of surprises, as this next account from Helen shows. She was hoping for a white feather, but her angels had a different plan.

Standing out

I have had several angel experiences myself – nothing dramatic but enough to help me out in difficult times. I would like to tell you about the latest one, which happened this week.

I am going through a tough time at the moment (it's too complicated to explain in detail). On Tuesday I was in a real state, so I asked my angel for a sign that she was there. I expected to find a white feather and was agitated that no white feather had appeared. Then a voice in my head told me to calm down by getting my knitting out and putting on a CD. I went to my CD rack and was astonished to find that one of my two angel CDs was the only one sticking out of a full rack of forty-five CDs. I have not listened to that CD for some time so there was no particular reason why it should have been sticking out. Also, I am a tidy person and my CDs are usually all neatly tucked in! I took this to be the sign I had asked for.

In this story the sign Arthur was hoping for also came from an unexpected source.

Some force

My story is concerning my mother, who I found dead in my apartment when she was on a visit to me. She had not been well and had a chest condition. Two nights before she passed away I heard her calling in her sleep, 'Molly', 'Daddy', but didn't think any more about it. It was not until later that I realised that her deceased sister Molly and her daddy must have been near to her in spirit as her time for passing over was drawing close. She was seventy-five years old when she passed and it was a traumatic experience for me but her doctor told me she had passed peacefully in her sleep.

I later cleared out her home and kept a little Swiss clock musical box that had belonged to her and that would play when you pulled the cord attached to the bottom. It had lovely Alpine decoration on the front and I put it on the wall of my bedroom. A few weeks later I was lying in bed reading, at around one in the morning, when it started to play of its own accord. I looked over to where it was on the wall, playing its little tune merrily away, and I said, 'Hi, Ma.' I got this most beautiful feeling of peace there in that bedroom. I got out of bed and walked over to the clock and I could hear the mechanism whirring away. There is no doubt that it had been activated by some force. It would be nice to think my mum was saying hello and that everything was OK where she was.

Susan's comforting sign also came in an unforeseen way at a time when she needed it the most. Here is her story.

The face of an angel

This last year has been a particularly hard and distressing one for me: since I lost my mother (looking after her until she passed on) I have for many years looked after my father as there is only me and him, no other family. This past year he has been in and out of hospital more than half a dozen times, each time becoming more weak and frail. At present I am caring for him for twenty-four hours a day, seven days a week, with very little rest. In the last two weeks it has been suggested to me that he will need to go into full-time care, and naturally I have been very upset at this, although I know it is the right way to go.

Anyway, this last week, as you are probably aware if you are in Britain at present, we have had exceptionally heavy snow, even in the south where I live, which is unusual. With all that has happened I have been praying for some guidance for my problems and all the decisions I need to make. I prayed that if the angels or spirits could hear me they would send me a sign to show me there really is something beyond this life. A little while later I looked out onto my snow-covered balcony and could not believe what I saw. I saw the face of a beautiful lady in the snow. Nobody could have put it there, as nobody has access to the balcony. It hadn't been there earlier although the snow had been there all day. I was so amazed I got one of my neighbours to look also and she said that she could see it even before I told her what to look for.

I enclose a photo I took of this face in the snow. Could it be that this is a way the angels have found to show me their presence?

I wrote back to Susan to tell her that there was no hesitation in my mind that this was a sign from heaven for her and also to thank her for the stunning photograph she sent to me. I have pinned it onto my angel picture board alongside other remarkable shots of angel faces in clouds, sand, mud, flowers and even toast. There really is no limit to the ways that angels can reveal their loving presence to us if our hearts are open to them.

Once again angels manifest in surprising ways in this next story, sent to me by Dorrie.

Angel dust

Here is my story: I was having my bathroom decorated so I took out every moveable item, washed it, then placed it on the bedroom floor. One of the items was a china owl. The next morning as the bathroom was ready I decided to put everything back and as I picked up the owl I noticed his head was covered in a circle of dust about a quarter of an inch thick, but there was no window open and the dust could not have come from the bedroom ceiling. It seemed to have appeared out of nothing. So I took the owl back to the bathroom and washed it again. I then went into the kitchen to make a cup of tea but in the corner of the sink was another perfect circle of dust – like a halo. Too amazed to think straight I washed it away.

Later I went into the living room where I have plants on the windowsill and there was yet another circle of dust on one of the plants. I cleared it away. As before, there was no dust on any surrounding items. When I told a friend about it, she smiled and told me it had to be angel dust. I was so sorry I had cleared it all away but there was a little left on the plant, so she could see I hadn't imagined it all. I felt very happy and honoured that this had happened, and many days I am aware of the angels' help. I am ninety-four years old and have quite a climb to go to the shops and each day I feel they help me – I seem to drift up the road.

Once again sceptics might say that the dust was simply house dust, but if that was the case why was the dust only to be found on the owl, the plant and in the sink? Yes, other explanations could be found, but what convinces me this was an angel calling card is that Dorrie told me she felt happy and honoured that this had happened. Positive feelings like this are always angel-inspired.

Many people have written to tell me that they find themselves inexplicably drawn towards buying a book or newspaper or magazine that they would not ordinarily buy and then finding that it features a story that is relevant to them in a powerful way. I like this story sent to me by Velma.

The star

I have to write and tell you what happened to me today – an angel coincidence. I went to the bookshop to get a book to read as I had run out, and saw one about angels. It was the last one left and I love reading books about spirits and angels and mediums so I bought it. I did not look at the author. Then I went to the newsagents to buy a newspaper and my TV guide for the week ahead. I usually buy the *Star* newspaper but I saw Amanda Holden on the front page of the *Mirror* and was saddened because I read she just lost her unborn baby so I bought that instead. When I got home, to my surprise there was an article about angels. I saw your name and read the article. Later that afternoon I took out the book I had bought at the bookshop and had to look twice – I could not believe it, you were the author! I bought the book first and then a newspaper about half an hour later that I never normally buy. Isn't that wonderful? I've sent you the receipt to prove it.

Many people have found themselves drawn to my books in this way, and whenever I get a letter like this one from Kerry-anne below it fills my heart with feelings of indescribable joy, honour and humility.

A new understanding

WOW! I started reading your book *An Angel Spoke to Me* and I am amazed at how once again I have a new understanding of life and death. Most of all I have a new understanding of me.

Recently I have been going through struggles with my mum and dad because of their drug addiction. I am always the one that tries to help them get their lives together again. Both have been addicted to drugs for a number of years and after many methadone prescriptions, a four-week stint in a rehabilitation centre and many a detox tried and tested, everything just seems to fail.

Recently my mum just seems to have gone further into herself. Talking to her is an issue now because she has started drinking to excess and any mention of this causes a great deal of guilt, which she cannot deal with. So instead of having a realistic conversation about it, she'll shout at a great volume and then leave. I am aware that she does this as a defence mechanism but I find it extremely frustrating. I feel like the one person I could talk to about anything has disappeared. I understand also that it's not my mum that's reacting in this way, it's the drugs and drink in her system talking. However, this does not change the feeling I have of being deserted.

Anyway, in November I had a phone call from my then boyfriend's ex-girlfriend explaining that he hadn't been faithful to me. Obviously it wasn't a nice phone call, and my boyfriend and I split up. I moved on and met my now boyfriend on Hogmanay. Weirdly we both weren't even meant to be at that party that night. A few months on from that I received a phone call from my brother (my brother and my ex are both in the military) explaining that my ex had been hit by an IED and was severely injured. For some reason I didn't feel anything, I just felt numb.

There is a point to why I am telling you all this: your book has been my guardian angel this time. The minute I started reading it a complete sense of relief came over me and a deeper meaning came to me from the words that you had written. Right from the start of the book I was crying one minute and laughing the next. There is a part right at the beginning of your book called 'The Desiderata' . . . oh my God, that is one powerful verse! It seemed to hit a part of me that I didn't realise existed.

Then I started reading your story about your childhood and some of your experiences and I felt overwhelmed at how much I share that loneliness and how anxious I become about people seeing the real me. But I started to see the real me. I started to see me as an individual that always seems to put everything on the line for everyone else, an individual that has a massive sense of awareness and yet never uses it to the best of her ability, a person that believes life isn't influenced by your past or even your future but influenced by you in the present, just by being. I realised that instead of worrying about my life failing I should just live day by day and treat each one as a rebirth in which I learn constantly about who I am on a deep inner level. It's whacked me like a lightning bolt . . . I can't change my mother, she has to be the one ready for change, and my energy could be used for much more important things.

You're probably wondering why I mentioned my ex . . . I realised something else for which I am forever grateful. It came to me that he and I weren't meant to be together; my angel noticed I was going through a rough time and called time on my relationship at the right time. Had it not been for my angel I would have been further down in the gutter worrying about him. My angel knew I was already having a tough time and saved me from any more hurt.

Through this my angel has taught me to love myself first and foremost and now I love this awesome man who has come into my life and he loves me back. We met that night for a reason, we were meant to be. Now we're looking forward to moving to England and starting a new life together later this year.

I realise this story is a bit all over the place, I just have that much to say that my mind's running away with itself. I sincerely thank you from the bottom of my heart for writing your books. I love how in each book you write the words just jump off the page and the story becomes real, giving people like me a realistic sense of just being, and enjoying the warmth of all those beautiful words.

Amy, whose story is below, believes she was guided to one of my books.

Guided

I'm currently reading your book *An Angel Spoke to Me*. It's the second book of yours I've read. The first was *An Angel Changed My Life*. I just wanted to say thank you so much for including the section in the former about hypersensitivity. It resonates so much and you can't imagine the relief it's brought me. Just to know there are others out there who are the same as me and really do understand means so much.

All my life, I've also been hypersensitive and have also experienced the things you outlined in the book. I'm happy to say that now, since going through several big life changes myself, I'm finally within the right circle of friends who I can connect with and who accept and love me for who I am. It's taken a long time to reach this point, but since entering the creative arenas in a voluntary capacity (I'm a volunteer radio presenter), I've found many like-minded and like-spirited people, which is just indescribable, really! Your book means so much to me, though, on a personal level, and reading the hypersensitivity section this morning actually brought tears of relief! So comforting and therapeutic to have somebody put it into words for us all to see. As you said, I was well and truly guided to that book, just as I was to the first one.

I've always allowed myself to be drawn naturally and intuitively to the right books and it works for me every time. I love to read anything I can find about angels and the spiritual realm. I'm incredibly drawn to all aspects of it and always welcome any opportunity to learn new things about it and meet new people who inspire me. I've had so many special experiences of the spiritual kind that I'd be here forever telling you about them all! I just love that I've had the chance to discover my gifts and use them to improve and enhance my life and, hopefully, those of others too. I'm still going through many difficult and challenging things and, in many ways, I'll have to go through some of them for the rest of my life, but I can honestly say that through the hardships and the darkness has come light and hope and better things and people.

I believe we all have a purpose in this life and that, one way or another, we'll find it. I really think, though, that books like yours help along the way. They always seem to come to me just at the right time, and I'm a strong believer in timing being of the utmost importance. Strangely enough, I seem to be being guided to say all this to you. I'd actually only intended to say thank you for that section of the book and something seems to have taken over. Apologies for overwhelming you with all this info, but it's coming from somewhere else and I don't seem to be able to stop it!

As you're reading this book now I'd like to think about how it came into your hands. Many people have written to me to tell me that one of my books was given to them by a friend or relative, or they went into a bookshop and were somehow drawn to it even though they had had no intention of buying an angel book. Or perhaps they literally stumbled across it or found it left behind on a Tube, bus or train. I no longer feel surprised at all when people tell me. Believe me, if you are reading this book now it found its way into your hands for a reason. Just like a white feather, a cloud, a butterfly or a coin, it is an angel calling card and you were guided to it and are meant to read it.

For Alison the sign she needed from above came in the form of a candle.

Lights in the darkness

I have just finished reading your book *An Angel Changed My Life*. I was drawn to it in the shop and loved reading it. Some stories made me cry. I would like to share with you my own angel experience.

Four years ago my nephew was born with cystic fibrosis; it's a serious, life-threatening condition that affects the lungs and bowels. He was in Great Ormond Street Hospital for three months; at one stage when he was in intensive care after his third operation the doctors told my sister he probably wouldn't survive the next twenty-four hours. She turned around and said, 'You don't know my son, he will get through this.' I was so upset. It was such a dark time in my life. I asked my husband if he thought our nephew would survive and he couldn't answer me. I needed an answer. I asked for a sign, I was so desperate to know.

When I left home that morning after asking for my sign, I looked up and there in the window was a single candle burning. I said, 'Thank you that is my sign that he is going to live.' I did feel very different after seeing that – I was more positive. My mother-in-law was staying with us and hadn't told me she was going to light a candle for my nephew every day.

Today my nephew is an active 4-year-old. We have a very close relationship, and I feel blessed that he is still with us. I am eternally grateful.

Others talk of hearing answers to their heartfelt questions when they turn on the radio or television or go online; sometimes they may even see the answers on stickers or posters on windows, on a bus or cab or on someone's T-shirt. Angels can also reveal themselves through the repeated appearance of certain numbers, most commonly the number 11, but any number or number sequence that has personal significance can be interpreted as an angel sign by those who believe. Then there are those wonderful stories I get from people who hear songs that have deep personal meaning playing on the car radio or in the background somewhere at just the right moment in their lives. The perfect timing of the song playing just when they needed to hear it the most convinces them that they are receiving a message from heaven.

Here's what happened to Lauren.

I have a dream

Hi Theresa – I have your new book in my hands and an experience that just made me laugh out loud to share with you. I picked up the book completely at random but something told me to get it, despite not really believing in angels and so on.

I have only just started reading the introduction and was interested to see that angels make their presence known by coincidences – something I have been experiencing a lot of lately. The most recent was on Friday while covering a court case – I was so bored (almost to tears) that I idly started listing how many Abba songs I knew. Yes, I was that bored. I recall thinking it would be easier if I had their Greatest Hits album!

Getting the train home, I saw that the service was delayed and went to the waiting room, where to my surprise they were playing an Abba song on the sound system. And the next song? More Abba. Yes, it was their Greatest Hits!

While I don't think this means the Swedish group has a special spiritual significance, only now while reading your book have I remembered the first song I heard in the waiting room. It was 'I Have a Dream' – and contains the line, 'I believe in angels'!

Hope you don't find that too convoluted – I just found it so funny that I was looking for meaning, and there it was!

Lauren found that her angel experience made her smile, and this is a sure sign for me that angels are close by. There is nothing your angels love more than to hear your laughter. Being spiritual does not mean always being serious and I've been sent many stories from people where the message is clear: our angels want us to lighten up because wherever there is honest laughter and joy heaven is never far away.

Signs of your angels at work can be found everywhere and anywhere. They are always trying to reach out to you and will often leave their messages in unique and personal ways that only make sense to you. These next two stories, the first from Deborah and the second from Fiona, show that sometimes it is a combination of signs and coincidences that point the way forward. It's a bit like a jigsaw puzzle – taken in isolation the pieces don't make sense, but when you put them all together a clear picture emerges.

Uncanny

My name is Deborah, and I had to email you to thank you for the wonderful book *An Angel Healed Me*. My friend read it recently and then lent it to me while I was recovering from an operation. So many things mentioned in the book remind me of experiences I have had, in particular the strange coincidences.

Robins appear to me at significant moments, whereas for my friend it is not robins but goldcrests, which she sees when people have died or at times of difficulty. She even found one on her doorstep just prior to her grandfather's death!

The inner voice is also something I can recognise; sometimes I ignore it and go ahead and do something the voice was saying not to, only to find out I ought to have paid attention. Alongside this, I sometimes get a churning feeling and instinctively know when something is wrong . . . that must be my own intuition. I too have dreamed of dead relatives and of estranged partners who I miss, and I've heard them speaking to me or felt them hugging me and showing sadness or remorse over our break-up. Until I read your book, I thought it might be wishful thinking, but these dreams seem to follow a sequence of seeing the person in my dream followed by the dream actually happening in real life . . . it's uncanny!

I don't want to ramble on, I just wanted to say how much comfort and hope your book has given me. I must finally though just tell you this: my friend who lent me her copy of your book has had a tough few years, as have I. She phones me often to share problems. About six weeks ago she rang me on my mobile while I was walking through my village. She was walking across her courtyard at work near Liverpool while we were chatting. I was telling her how fabulous your book was and how it had comforted me and I mentioned the white feathers and how I do see them a lot at certain times. At that exact moment I saw one on the footpath right in front of me, and at the exact same moment she squealed and said that she had just picked one up off the ground in front of her. It was unbelievable to both find a white feather at EXACTLY the same instant while chatting on our mobiles about feathers. I took a picture on my phone to prove I had indeed found one . . . it seemed so contrived that I doubted anyone would believe this. It's possibly one of the most astonishing things I have encountered, but there are many things I recall which I believe have to be more than just coincidences, and dreams which were more than just dreams.

The most wonderful feeling

My name is Fiona and I shall start at the beginning: on 2 August 2010, after not being able to contact my partner at his home, I decided to head from Newcastle to Sunderland straight to his place. I knew when I got off the bus and walked to his home that things were not right. His curtains were semi-open, the way I had left them the day before. I then took a deep breath and opened his front door. Hearing the TV on I shouted 'Barry!' and then went into his sitting room, where I found him. My soul mate had died of a massive heart attack. This was a total shock to me as, although I was forty years old, I had never seen a dead body. I was inconsolable, absolutely shattered. We had had an extremely happy relationship. We did not live together but would text and ring each other every day.

Not long after, days maybe, I started to experience what I thought were strange coincidences, but I now believe I was being comforted by a spiritual force. It was at this time that I started to write down these coincidences and signs, and believe me there were plenty, and I started to feel like I was not alone. For example, my Barry was a Geordie and a huge Newcastle United fan, so he was a 'magpie'. Just after he died I was sitting in my garden writing my eulogy to him when I heard a magpie singing its heart out for ages in a tree next door. It made me feel Barry was watching over me. Ever since then I often see magpies – I didn't before – and often it is a lone magpie coming into my garden and chirping away.

Anyway, one day after the funeral I was finding life extremely difficult and painful. I was feeling utterly heartbroken when suddenly I experienced the most wonderful sensation. I was leaning on the patio door handles when I felt a warm pressure on the back of my shoulder. No one was with me, but it lasted approximately five to ten seconds. I know it was my guardian angel letting me know I was not alone. Over the last few months since Barry died, whenever I think about him or miss him, I am often visited by magpies. I will also hear music that he loved on the radio, like 'Owner of a Lonely Heart' by Yes, or I switch the television on and they will be showing Spitfires, for example on the anniversary of the Battle of Britain – he loved those planes.

It was around October 2010, when I was in a café with my mum and sister, that I picked up the *Daily Mail* and there was an article inside about guardian angels. They were talking about your book, *An Angel Changed My Life*. I could not leave until I had read the article, and then just before Christmas 2010, yet another wonder-ful coincidence. I went to get a prescription from my doctor and called into the library beforehand, and lo and behold, there in the new book section was your book. I immediately got it and the stories

I read made me feel inspired and overwhelmed but also extremely comforted and at peace.

All the signs mentioned in this chapter – and indeed this book – are messages from heaven, but never forget that angels don't restrict themselves to feathers or coincidences or dreams or numbers. If you look at the world through angel eyes you can find them in everyone and everything, from music to rainbows, clouds to dewdrops, kisses to the lyrics of a song, and from every act of kindness to every positive thought. Angels can be felt in every atom of the universe and beyond. They are part of the interconnection between this world and the next, which all those with a sensitive heart, a Celtic heart, can see and feel.

And the more you think about angels and ask them to reveal themselves to you, the more likely they are to appear. All you need to do is keep an open mind because, as you've seen, angels and the spirits of departed loved ones will reveal themselves in the most surprising and unexpected ways. This spectacular story, sent to me by Josephine, illustrates this yet again.

The silver firework

I've decided to write and tell you about an amazing experience I had very recently. My dad died in December 2010. Unfortunately we had been estranged and out of touch for fourteen years. My dad split from my mum and remarried and moved to another part of the country. When I found out he had died I was shocked and very upset, not having had a chance to get back in touch after so long and not being able to say goodbye.

In the week leading up to his funeral I travelled up to the chapel of rest to see Dad and say goodbye. I went with one of my brothers. I told Dad I forgave him for everything and that I was sorry too.

Around that time and before the funeral, when I was crying and by myself, I asked my dad out loud for a sign – any sign to tell me there was an afterlife and that that is where we go on to. At the cremation my family and I met my dad's wife for the first time. Everything just seemed so surreal and it was very painful. Dad didn't get a chance to meet any of my three children and had lost touch with four of his own. After the cremation and wake the last thing my dad's wife said was, 'We have to hope your dad is looking down on us from somewhere.' I said I believed he was.

After that I travelled back home with my husband in the back of my brother's car – his wife was driving. It was dark but a clear night. We set off around 6.30 p.m. and I felt calm, knowing the worst was over and I was going home to my children. Around 7 p.m. I was looking out of the window when a silver firework shot up into the sky. I watched it, waiting for it to explode – it didn't. The top of the firework, hazy at first, changed into a shimmering gold cross. It was solid and bright and real. The cross was held up by the silver beam of light that had been the firework. I kept my eyes firmly on it and as we travelled past I turned round and looked for it – it was still there. I did not imagine this, and I could not have imagined anything like this happening. To me it felt like a vision or revelation. There were no other fireworks going off, and for it to happen when and how it did still amazes me and gives me goose-bumps when I think about it. I feel as if someone or something was giving me the answer to the question I had asked about the afterlife.

I know it definitely happened, and I will never forget it. I feel I was shown something amazing and extraordinary from another realm. I feel blessed to have witnessed it. My vision answered the question I had but I also feel it taught me a few things. It felt like being shown a sign of forgiveness. I do not have lots of happy memories of growing up when Dad was around so it's all quite painful. However, he was my dad and I forgave him and somehow maybe he forgave me and wanted me to know that yes, there is an afterlife and he had arrived, and the silver firework was a celebration of him arriving.

This chapter has talked about a number of angel calling cards but I don't think it would be complete – indeed this book would not be complete – without talking about another special way that angels frequently choose to reach out to us, and that is through the patience, love, trust and devotion of animals. Many people have written to me over the years to tell me they believe the unconditional love of their pets connects them to a higher force. Pam's story is a lovely example.

Protected

Some years ago now we had a lovely Labrador called Jimmy; at that time we also kept racing pigeons. After his puppy stage Jimmy used to live in his comfortable kennel in the garden. His dwelling was his castle. He was such a knowing dog, and gentle; when his breakfast of cereal and warm milk was presented, the young pigeons would enquire what was happening, and Jimmy would sit and watch them eat some of his breakfast, then he would carry on when they were finished! On racing days he instinctively knew when one of ours was going to 'fly in'; he would keep incredibly still until the pigeon had been 'clocked'. He also knew the next-door neighbour kept dog biscuits and would wander into his kitchen and sit by the cupboard until Bill obliged.

I loved him so much as the years went by. My husband and Jimmy used to have rough-and-tough wrestles but Jimmy also looked after me. One day when Jimmy was twelve years old he was just staying very quiet by my side as I pottered about the place; then when it was nearly time for my husband to return from work Jimmy walked to the back gate. He moved to one side as Mick drove into the garden, and as soon as Mick alighted from the van Jimmy looked up at him and started an horrendous yelping, squealing and turning. I was mortified, as was Mick. He said he was taking Jimmy straight to the vet. I had a part-time job in a nursing home at the time, so I hugged them both and hoped Jimmy would be OK. When I returned home from work the house was silent and my husband was very upset. I asked where Jimmy was; the vet had found he was riddled with cancer and had put him to sleep.

I strongly believe Jimmy deliberately awaited Mick's return from work, to let him handle the situation because he knew I wouldn't have been able to.

A couple of years after Jimmy's demise we adopted a bull terrier cross from the kennels. He was about three years old. He settled in very quickly and we named him Freddy; he was a toughie and always looked after me, and I would take him for a walk every day. One day Freddy and I were walking through the woods near the park. Normally, he would have a sniff around then come back, but this particular day he would not leave my side, despite my insistence for him to explore; then he just suddenly but slowly sat down, growling deeply and staring ahead; as I looked up a man was exposing himself. Freddy began to show his top teeth but remained by my side. The man ran off and I was obviously shaken but glad I had Freddy looking out for me.

Like angels, beloved pets love us and watch over us in this life, and it is not surprising that many people believe that this love doesn't end when their pet dies. I have had so many letters from people who believe their departed pets are watching over them in spirit that it is impossible to ignore the phenomenon.

Gill believes her dog is still with her.

Clicking claws

I do believe that spirits stay with us. Two years ago our dog Oscar of thirteen years died of cancer just before Christmas. The night after he died both my husband and I swear we heard his claws clicking across the kitchen floor. Since then I have often felt him behind me. We now have a Westie called Murray and he sometimes just stops in the middle of the room staring at me and will come nowhere near me. Then he shakes his head and bounds over laughing. I am convinced that Oscar is next to me and Murray is giving me time with him.

Even those who believe in an afterlife for human spirits may be dismissive of animal ghosts or spirits. It is often said that animals don't have souls or spirits, so they cannot survive death as humans may do, but animals are made of the same energy that humans are and in my mind there is no reason why they may not survive in the same way. Anyone who has ever bonded with their pet will be aware of the strong, sometimes psychic, connection that can exist between human and animal. Psychic energy could very possibly be part of the same energy as spiritual energy and so animals could have as much connection to the world of spirit as humans. Perhaps more so, given their often superior senses of taste, smell, sight and hearing and their ability to sense what is unseen.

I truly believe that love, whether in human or animal form, can cross the boundaries of time and space, and many people who have lost beloved pets believe that their animals continue to visit them in spirit. After my first cat Crystal died, I would often sense her presence or feel the brush of her body against my legs. I was never frightened by these experiences – quite the contrary they seemed the most comforting and natural thing in the world. And the more stories I hear from people who have had similar experiences the more convinced I am that contact with a beloved deceased pet is possible. For me and others, it's clear that distance and even death cannot break the psychic bond between human and animal.

Angel believes her cat came back for one last goodbye.

Burning bright

Tiger was my baby. She was the most stunningly beautiful Persian cross you can imagine. She also had the loudest purr you could imagine – now I know why they call them purrsians. I lived with Tiger and loved her every second of the five years we spent together, but she got very ill and needed to be put to sleep.

One morning I was sitting in my chair drinking my tea and watching breakfast TV when I felt something jump onto the back of the sofa and brush past my neck. Then I felt something kneading my left shoulder. Tiger always used to do that when she was alive. It was part of our morning ritual. I also felt warmth, happiness and light all around me. I wasn't daydreaming or dreaming. I didn't imagine it. Tiger came back for one last goodbye.

One of the most heart-warming things about a visitation by a spirit pet is the promise that this isn't really a goodbye at all and one day there will be a reunion in the afterlife, as described so fondly in the well-known story of the Rainbow Bridge – a mythical place inspired by a poem first published in the 1980s. In this poem the spirit of a beloved pet departs to a sunny meadow where it plays happily until reunited with its owner in death. When the owner's death is close the pet senses this and before owner and pet go to heaven together there is an emotional meeting between the two.

Kylie's story shows how animals can sometimes send us unexpected messages of hope and comfort from the other side.

Made me cry

My auntie gave birth to a baby girl eleven years ago but sadly the baby didn't make it past two days old.

My auntie told me that just the other day she was out and a lady with a dog came up to her and said, 'I don't know why but my dog wanted to come over and say hello to you. She has never done that before.' This dog had a pattern of a cross on its back. My auntie was talking to the lady and asked what her dog's name was. She said, 'Nikki.' My auntie was astonished and told the lady about her own Nikki, her baby girl Nikita who had died.

My auntie knew it was her little girl coming to say hello. It made her cry and it made me cry too.

Gillian shares her moving tale.

Never apart

My wonderful, wonderful dog Bettanie died on the 19 November 2004. She and I were more than just a dog and human companion. We loved each other. In the ten years she lived we were apart just two weeks and I never got bored or fed up with her company. I never even had to tell her off. At two years she started to have fits. It was to lead to eight years of illness for her, but she didn't give in and neither did I. We shared bad times but also good times and the good times were the best times of my life. We had so much fun and I would even say we were very alike.

In August this year we had to remember the anniversary of my mum's death. I really didn't want to go over all the pain in my mind again but we lit candles and laughed at things we remembered. It was a fairly ordinary day but that night I had the most strange and amazing experience. I don't know where I was. I wasn't in my bedroom. I wasn't anywhere, but I was holding Bett's head in my hands and I kissed her on the side of her face as I used to. She closed her little eyes as she used to. I could feel the weight of her head in my hands, the thick fur against my neck. I could even smell her breath on my face. I could smell her and feel the bony structure of her face as I kissed her. I could feel her presence, but most of all I could feel such a profound feeling of love and peace. I woke up in the morning and wondered if it had been real.

It didn't dawn on me until a few days later that I hadn't remembered the anniversary of Bett's passing as I had done for the last six years. But the night I had been grieving my mum my Bettanie had come to comfort me.

And now Sue shares hers . . .

True love

I lost Beau, my dog and true love, in January 2010. My sixtieth birthday was 7 February and my daughter had booked lunch at a restaurant for us. I asked my friend Jenny to dog-sit our other little dog, Laura, while we were out. When we returned, Jenny seemed rather upset. Eventually she told us that after we had gone out she went into the kitchen to make a cup of tea and when she turned round, there lying on the sofa, looking well and totally real, was Beau! She said, 'Hello, Beau,' and he looked at her and then went. I knew that he had come back because it was my birthday. He always waited for me in the kitchen and would not move. It gave me great comfort. I have since heard him, smelled his sweet, baby smell, and seen shadows where he used to lie. It gives me such comfort.

They may not be angels in the traditional sense, but with their empathy, patience, devotion and unconditional love, beloved pets sound a lot like angels to me. Like angels, they simply love us and watch over us in this life and the next.

And it's not just pets that can walk beside us as angels – I've also been sent angel stories about wild animals, birds and even insects. Remember, in Celtic spirituality everyone and everything carries with it a blessing, and that includes all living creatures. I'd like to conclude here with this story sent to me by Malcolm.

Pecking order

It couldn't have been worse timing for me to take a day off work to look after my 2-year-old son Gary. I had a deadline I had to meet, but my wife, who normally looked after Gary, was laid up with flu and her mum was on holiday and we didn't really have any babysitters.

I spent all morning trying to exhaust Gary so that I could work in the afternoon. I felt pretty tense singing nursery rhymes and playing hide and seek while my colleagues were up to their necks in work. I needed to be there, but my place was with my son. Eventually I did wear him down and after a big lunch he fell asleep on the living room sofa while watching TV. I covered him with a blanket and seized the moment to escape to my home office.

I had been busy on my laptop for quite a while when I was interrupted by this high-pitched sound. It startled me. I looked around and noticed that there was a robin sitting on the window-sill, chirping and warbling with all its might. This was so unusual and enchanting that I was mesmerised. Birds usually fly away from me as I'm quite a big fellow but this one could clearly see me and was not at all shy. After a while the bird got so agitated that I got up to check that it wasn't injured. I got really close to it and still it didn't fly away. It just chirped harder. Then when I reached forward to open the window it bounced down from the ledge and started hopping and fluttering around on the grass. I had so much work to do and so little time to do it but this first robin sighting of the spring was so enchanting I didn't want it to end. I decided to go out into the garden to watch it a bit more and perhaps even feed it some breadcrumbs.

I went to the back door in the kitchen and that's when I heard another startling sound. This time it was splashing sounds and they were coming from the paddling pool I'd filled in the morning to splash around in with Gary. I ran outside and saw to my horror that Gary was in the pool. He must have woken up and gone outside by himself. He wasn't in any danger but there is no telling what might have happened if he had stayed in the water unattended for longer. I pulled him out and crushed him to my chest, cursing my thoughtless-ness in not locking the back door. Was this rescue robin an angel? I don't know, because I never saw it again. I just keep my eyes and ears open now to the signs nature sends me.

I hope the stories you've been reading have shown you that there may very well have been times in your life when you entertained angels unaware and – as the final chapter of this book will explain – never is this more true than when it comes to stories of angels working through other people.

CHAPTER SEVEN

Angel Inspirations

May the blessings of light be upon you
Light without and within you
And in all your comings and goings
May you ever have a kindly greeting
From those you meet along the road

Irish Angel Blessing for the road

The ancient Celts recognised the power of community to transform and inspire lives and I'm going to conclude this book by
talking about perhaps the most powerful of all ways that angels
can speak to us, and that is when they work through our fellow
human beings.

Earlier we looked at stories about mysterious strangers who
somehow appear at just the right time with the right kind of
help and then vanish afterwards, leaving the person involved
wondering if they actually encountered an angel in human
form. In this last group of stories it is pretty clear that these
are not cases of angels appearing in human form but cases of

humans doing the work of angels. But to the person involved, the impact on their lives is just as powerful because it restores their faith in the life-changing power of love and kindness.

Let's begin with this story sent to me by Sheila.

Road works

It was early one Saturday morning and I was travelling from Bognor Regis in Sussex to Egham in Surrey for a yoga conference. I am a yoga teacher so it was important for me to get there on time. I had reached Milford, a few minutes before the junction to get me onto the busy A3 road. It's a road that is always busy as it leads directly onto the M25.

The road I was on was reasonably quiet for a Saturday morning, but suddenly my car went completely out of control! There was no way I could hold it steady, the car did a complete U-turn and ended up facing the way I had just come on the opposite side of the road. I felt very shaken, as this had never happened to me before. I got out to look at the damage and I still didn't know what had caused the car to go out of control like that. I thought it must have been a puncture. At the same time a white van suddenly appeared and three men in dirty white overalls jumped out and came over to see what they could do. They said they saw me when the car left the road and when they realised it was a puncture they simply said, 'Not to worry.' They took the spare wheel out of the boot and had the jack in operation and the tyre changed in less than ten minutes. I was amazed, it had all happened so quickly. I told them they were angels, thanked them and asked if they would take something to get themselves a drink. They refused, got in their van and were gone before I had even turned the car around.

I continued my journey and a few minutes later I went over the junction onto the A3 and just could not believe my eyes. What is normally a busy dual carriageway running past Guildford was reduced to two lanes due to road works. The two lanes were packed solid. I then realised just how lucky I had been. If the puncture had happened a few minutes later, on this stretch of road with the amount of traffic there was on it there would have been a most horrifying crash. Reaction then set in and I started to tremble at the thought of the narrow escape I'd had.

If those three men were not angels themselves then they were obviously sent by my guardian angel or maybe my husband. I don't know! He used to be a coach driver so knew that stretch of road well. I am just very grateful that someone was looking after me that day.

And now this one sent to me by Lorna.

Sent to comfort me

I thought I would send you an email as I have just read your book *An Angel Changed My Life*! I have also just ordered another four of your books as I was so inspired by the first one I read, which was a gift from my daughter.

I was reading your book on holiday in Spain over Christmas. My aunt died the first day I arrived on my holiday and when I got the news I couldn't find my partner, but I bumped into a really nice man, who to me was an angel. This man knew I was upset and stayed with me and helped me find my partner, who had slipped out of the hotel to get some cigarettes. I will never forget his kindness and how he comforted me. I had been through a bad few years as my ex-partner was dying from cirrhosis of the liver and cancer, which he would not accept or do anything to help himself. While I was on holiday he also died and I found out on Christmas Day. The same man (and his wife) comforted me at this time again. On the last day of our holidays we all got together and found that the four or us really hit it off and that we all believed in angels! I had the most fantastic talk with them and we exchanged email addresses. I really believe they were sent to comfort me at this time as I was far from home.

Jane also believes angels can manifest their love through other people.

Early hours

I'm not sure if what happened to me was a visit by an angel or not; I will tell you what happened and maybe you will be able to tell me.

In February 2010 I had to rush my mother into hospital in the early hours of the morning as she had an abdominal swelling and a high temperature and was going into shock. She was admitted onto a ward and, after seeing her settled, I went back home. She was in hospital for fourteen days and in all that time I was going to work (I work early mornings so was getting up at 4.30 a.m.), dashing home quickly, getting changed and going up to the hospital, then after visiting I was coming home, sorting out the washing, doing the ironing, tidying round the house, seeing to our two cats then going back to the hospital for evening visiting . . . as you might imagine I was very tired.

One day, I was sitting on my checkout when a lady said, 'Are you having a bad day, Jane?' I didn't know this person but told her that I was just so tired as my mother was in hospital and I was dashing here and there with no time for anything, and she said if I wanted any washing, shopping or cleaning done – in fact anything at all – to just get in touch with her. She said, 'I'm not just saying it, I mean it, anything, even if you just want to talk.' I said thank you and told her that I would burst into tears if she said any more; in fact my eyes have filled with tears as I relate this to you now. She leaned across my counter and gave me a hug. I have never encountered anyone so kind before or since and I have never seen this lady again.

Was this just someone who was very kind or was it an angel letting me know that I was not alone and help was there if I asked for it? Must sign off now as this still deeply affects me and I always cry.

Ignatius believes that the world is full of Good Samaritans because he has met them.

Good Samaritans

We drove from Sydney to Canberra for an art exhibition. The ticket to the exhibition was $30. We were four adults and two children – six tickets (with the children charged half price) would cost $150. As my son stood in the ticket queue, he was approached by an old couple who had two extra tickets. Despite his repeated requests for them to accept money for the tickets, they refused. Not wanting to hurt a generous couple, my son gratefully accepted the gift. He saved $60. Why did the couple single him out of so many in the queue? Why would they not accept money? It is still a puzzle.

On another occasion we were on a long-distance trip when the fuel gauge in the car stopped working. Hoping to refill at the next town, I continued to drive. Miles down the highway, the car stopped – the fuel tank was empty. We stood by the side of the car waiting for help. Minutes later, a man rode past on his two-wheeler, looked at us and turned around to enquire if we were stranded for want of fuel. Without our even asking, he emptied the fuel he had with him in a can into our vehicle. He said he would ride back to the fuel station and collect more fuel for himself. Why did the Good Samaritan stop? Why did he give us the fuel he needed? There are no answers to these questions, only an assumption that he was an angel sent to help us.

Anne also believes angels were sent to help her. Like many people who have encountered unexpected kindness she often wonders if she encountered something otherworldly. Perhaps she did. Read her story and see what you think.

Sent to help us

I have a phobia about getting lost – I even have nightmares about being in big cities on my own and lost. Last year we were in Montreal on holiday, totally and utterly lost. We had arrived by coach with a group we had joined at the airport. We had started walking early in the evening and after we had walked for a while it started to get dark. There were plenty of police around as there had been a local ice hockey match and they were expecting unrest, but as they had been brought in from other cities they were unfamiliar with the area and couldn't help.

We'd stopped to try and decide what to do and a couple of about the same age as us were walking towards us smiling, as if they knew us. We didn't know them but assumed they recognised us from the tour group. We had joined an escorted tour from Toronto and were to be with the same tour group for the whole of the holiday.

As they reached us I said, 'Are you staying at the same hotel as us?' and the woman said, with a Scottish accent, 'What hotel would that be then?' I told her it was The Mirage, and she said (looking at a little map she had in her hand), 'You're going the wrong way, it's this way.' So we walked together back in the other direction. We chatted along the way and the couple said they were from Sterling in Scotland and that they were flying back to Manchester on the same day as us. We got back to the hotel and went in, while they walked on, saying they were just going for a drink before bed.

We got talking to other people on the tour and nobody remembered the Scottish couple. We never saw them again, either at the hotel, on the tours, on the coach back to the airport, on the plane, at baggage reclaim – in fact, apart from the half hour they guided us back to our hotel, we had never seen them before and did not see them since. Were this couple angels in human form sent to help us? I think so.

Wouldn't it be wonderful if we lived our lives with an awareness of the heavenly potential that exists within not just ourselves but others? Wouldn't it be wonderful if we were always wondering what blessings our fellow human beings bring with them? In such a world there would be no such thing as a stranger. And it's not just through adults that angels can reveal themselves to us – they often choose to express themselves through our children. There is a special closeness between children and angels because children tend to be naturally intuitive, spontaneous and open-minded, and therefore more open to the divine interconnectedness of things. Gill's story is fairly typical – if anything is typical as far as angels are concerned – of those I receive from parents with sensitive children.

Old soul

When my son was younger he would often talk animatedly to himself in his room. He told me that he was chatting with his brothers and sisters that I had lost. He is now sixteen and he has told me that when he fell asleep as a child he would see flashing lights in the room. When he was a toddler I used to joke that he had an old soul. We were once walking through a graveyard when he was about three. He stopped in front of a gravestone and clearly said, 'It is very sad here,' then bowed his head and moved on.

Many children seem aware of layers of existence that quite simply confuse or astonish adults. Being fresh from heaven, the possibility is strong that they are more open to contact with spirits and angels, but, in much the same way that you don't need to have Celtic blood to see angels, you don't need to lose that special connection with angels as you grow up. Indeed, with an open heart and mind it can grow stronger. Whether we are nine or ninety there is still a child in each of us that has always believed in miracles, and when we rediscover that child we realise that we haven't really grown old at all.

This next story involves a child and was well reported by the media at the time. As you'll see, it isn't about a child with angel eyes, but about a woman with the heart and courage of an angel. You may well remember the story but it is so wonderful I want to paraphrase it here.

Divine rescue

A British woman on holiday in Orlando has been hailed a guardian angel by the parents of 16-month-old Jah-Nea Myles, who fell from the fourth-floor balcony of a hotel.

Helen Beard, forty-four, from Worksop, Nottinghamshire, spotted the child dangling through the balcony as she relaxed beside a pool at the Econo Lodge Inn & Suites. She ran to the spot directly under Jah-Nea, who is thought to have hit the balcony below on her way down, which broke her fall. Although she slipped from Helen's arms and did hit the ground, according to police reports, Mrs Beard's actions saved the child's life and she did not sustain any serious injuries.

Authorities investigating the incident described the rescue as a miracle and it just goes to show heroes are normal people who are capable of doing extraordinary things. The child's mother, who had left the toddler in the care of friends and did not notice she had slipped out of the room until she heard screaming, is quoted as saying: 'Not a scratch on her body. I'm thanking the Lord above right now for saving my child's life. I'm also thanking that lady because she was an angel sent from heaven.'

And it is not always dramatic acts of courage or quick thinking that can save lives – sometimes simple acts of kindness or a few well-chosen words are enough, as this next story submitted to a *Sunday Post* letters page and sent to me by Charlotte shows.

Angel on an Italian island

While visiting the church on an Italian Island I came across some children leaving notes on the board for loved ones who had passed on. A little girl asked me to pin her note up because she couldn't reach. She said thank you and explained the note was for her daddy.

'It's my birthday soon,' she explained, 'and he said he would buy me a special baby doll, but we've moved to a new house so I've sent him my new address.' When she left the church I could not resist having a peep at her note and making a note of her birthday and her address. I bought her the sweetest doll I could find and sent it with a note explaining that because there were no shops in heaven I had done her daddy's shopping for him. I signed my letter, 'From the lady who pinned your note on the board in the church on the island.'

We can all be aspiring angels like the lady who visited the church on that Italian island and we can all offer compassion, kindness and love that can help others feel as if their lives have been touched by the angels. And if it isn't possible to give practical help, we can always send our loving thoughts, as research has shown that there really is healing power in positive emotional energy which some call prayer.

This next lovely story, which is on the internet, is a great reminder that life really can be beautiful and that there's potentially an angel in all of us.

Dead letters

Our 14-year-old dog Abbey died last month. The day after she died, my 4-year-old daughter Meredith was crying and talking about how much she missed Abbey. She asked if we could write a letter to God so that when Abbey got to heaven, God would recognise her. I told her that I thought we could, so she dictated these words:

Dear God,

Will you please take care of my dog? She died yesterday and is with you in heaven. I miss her very much. I am happy that you let me have her as my dog even though she got sick.

I hope you will play with her. She likes to play with balls and to swim. I am sending a picture of her so when you see her you will know that she is my dog. I really miss her.

Love,

Meredith

We put the letter in an envelope with a picture of Abbey and Meredith and addressed it to God/Heaven. We put our return address on it. Then Meredith pasted several stamps on the front of the envelope because she said it would take lots of stamps to get the letter all the way to heaven. That afternoon she dropped it into the letter-box at the post office. A few days later, she asked if God had got the letter yet. I told her that I thought He had.

Yesterday, there was a package wrapped in gold paper on our front porch addressed 'To Meredith' in an unfamiliar hand. Meredith opened it. Inside was a book by Mr Rogers called *When a Pet Dies*. Taped to the inside front cover was the letter we had written to God in its opened envelope. On the opposite page was the picture of Abbey and Meredith and this note:

Dear Meredith,

Abbey arrived safely in heaven. Having the picture was a big help. I recognised Abbey right away.

Abbey isn't sick anymore. Her spirit is here with me just like it stays in your heart. Abbey loved being your dog. Since we don't need our bodies in heaven, I don't have any pockets to keep your picture in, so I am sending it back to you in this little book for you to keep and have something to remember Abbey by. Thank you for the beautiful letter and thank your mother for helping you write it and sending it to me. What a wonderful mother you have. I picked her especially for you. I send my blessings every day and remember that I love you very much. By the way, I'm easy to find, I am wherever there is love.

Love,

God

Angels can exist within each one of us. The kind soul at the post office who wrote the letter could easily have ignored it and been a jobsworth, but instead he chose to make a difference. Indeed, one of the most powerful ways to see angels is to discover them from within. Many of us have no idea that everything we feel, say and do has the potential to bring a glimpse of heaven to others. Whenever you feel love or go out of the way for someone you are being an angel. A simple act of kindness can help someone find comfort or beauty in their life and a kind or gentle word can bring sunshine into the lives of others. You may think that one small kind deed is pointless or ineffectual when there is so much injustice and pain in the world, but let me assure you that in the world of spirit any heartfelt thought, word or action has great power.

I can think of no better way to illustrate this point than with one of my all-time favourite wisdom stories. This story has been circulated in many versions, usually with no mention of an author. It is said to be paraphrased from 'The Star Thrower' by Loren Eiseley (1907–1977).

Starfish

It was still early. The mist had not yet cleared from the sea.

In the distance, a solitary figure stood throwing objects out over the water. Walking along the debris-strewn beach, I looked at the masses of starfish scattered everywhere. The tide had thrown them in, stranding them on the beach. As the sun rose higher, they would perish.

Approaching the stranger, I could see that it was the starfish he was picking up and returning to the sea. Our eyes met.

'Do you really think you can help? There are millions of starfish on this beach. You can help so few. Does it really make a difference? Does it matter?'

He reached down and picked up another starfish, looking at it intently.

'Oh yes,' he replied. 'It matters to this one!'

As human beings, we should become aware that we are all gifted with the ability to make a difference. We have the power to changes the lives of others for the better. We must each find our starfish and throw our stars wisely. We can all make a very real difference in the world. Each day there are opportunities to make someone else's life easier and I truly believe that easing the hearts and minds of others not only feeds our spirits but also strengthens our connection with the angels. At this point I am going to place this short but perfect parable. I find myself forever returning to it in my writing and in my life as it never fails to inspire and motivate me.

The boy in the street

I was walking home one day and came across a tiny boy cold and shivering in a threadbare pair of shorts and a ragged shirt. He was sitting on the side of the street and his eyes were filled with despair. I got so angry and asked my guardian angel, 'Why do you allow things like this to happen? Why don't you intervene and help him?'

My angel replied, 'I am doing something about it. I brought you here.'

If you think you can only find angels around you or in the actions of others, this story is a potent reminder that angels exist within each one of us. If you don't think you can see your angels working their magic in your life, the fastest and best way to discover them is from the inside out. We can all be angels in disguise, bringing laughter and comfort to those who cross our paths. If we could all reach out to help one another from time to time, and teach this way of life to our children, imagine the angelic impact this would have on the world. Imagine how much easier it would be for our angels to work with, for and through us.

Irish Angel Blessings
May you have:
A world of wishes at your command.
God and his angels close to hand.
Friends and family their love impart,
and Irish blessings in your heart!

Those with Celtic hearts can teach us a great deal about finding angel blessings in every aspect of our lives, even in our hair! Sadly, though, we live in a materialistic, cynical world, and there is so much pressure on us to be rational, logical and doubting. Of course, we all need to be rational at times and not believe everything we are told, but if our hearts draw us towards angels and tell us to do the right or positive thing, we should not try to fight it or rationalise it. Angels have a way of speaking to us in deeply personal, often unexplainable ways, and just as what matters at the end of our lives on earth is how much we have loved, at the end of the day what truly matters is what our hearts tell us.

To welcome angels into your life, all you need to do is silence your fears and open up a conversation with heaven. If you reach out in this way, with an open and trusting heart, your guardian angel will be there to inspire and guide you through all the wonders, challenges and possibilities waiting for you in this life and the next.

I can't promise that living with your angels will always be easy – how could you learn and grow if everything came easily to you? – but I can promise you that any challenges, losses and sorrows you face will become easier to cope with when you know that you are never alone, however lost you may feel.

Your angels are here to remind you that you are a beloved child of the universe and that this life is a wonderful journey that does not end with death. So try to open your heart to the angels around and within you and to think positively about yourself and others. In this way you will be helping to bring the angels closer to earth and when the moment comes for you to leave this world behind, you will not only have left it a lighter and brighter place but you will be soaring without guilt, fear or regret to your new home in spirit. Some people call this home nirvana, others call it heaven, but whatever name you call it it is a place of peace, love and light where angels reside.

Don't forget, angels can appear in countless different ways and even if you aren't quite sure that they are real, they don't disappear. Those born with Celtic blood running through their veins may have a natural affinity with angels, but each and every one of us has a guardian angel walking beside us, waiting for the moment when we find the courage to open our hearts and let our inner angel reach up to heaven. And the moment, the very instant we do that, we attract love, magic, laughter and miracles into our lives.

There is nothing complicated or difficult about it at all. You do not need to be psychic, or saintly, or Irish to connect with heaven. There are no preconditions. Angels are divine messengers whose essence is love and light, and they are for everyone and everything. All you need to do is ask, and when you open yourself to their guidance and their message you evolve spiritually by creating heaven on earth within. You instinctively understand or remember something you always knew but with the pressures and routines of daily life had somehow forgotten along the way: you are not a human being having a spiritual experience but a spiritual being having a human experience.

Yes, you are human, but you are also so much more. In truth, you are a spiritual being in physical form. Don't try to be perfect – that can wait until you are in heaven – down here on earth you have much to learn as you try to love yourself and others unconditionally. You are both mortal and eternal and, as the ancient Celts recognised all those centuries ago, you have an existence far beyond this life and you are far greater than you think you are.

And with that life-changing thought it is time for me to sign off now – but before I do I just want to wish you love, magic and Irish angel blessings on your remarkable journey through this life and into the next.

About the Author

Theresa Cheung is the author of a variety of books including the *Sunday Times* bestsellers *An Angel Called My Name, An Angel on My Shoulder* and *Angel Babies*. She is also the author of the international bestseller *The Element Encyclopedia of 20,000 Dreams, The Element Encyclopedia of the Psychic World* and the top ten *Sunday Times* bestseller *An Angel Healed Me*, as well as *An Angel Changed My Life, How to See Your Angels* and *An Angel Spoke to Me*. Theresa's books have been translated into twenty different languages and her writing has featured in *Chat – It's Fate, Spirit & Destiny, Prediction, Red* and *Prima* magazines, as well as the *Daily Express, Daily Mail* and *Sunday Times Style*. In addition, Theresa has worked on books for Derek Acorah, Yvette Fielding, Tony Stockwell and Dr William Bloom. Born into a family of psychics and spiritualists, Theresa has been involved in the research of psychic phenomena for over twenty-five years since gaining a Masters from King's College, Cambridge. She has also been a student at the College of Psychic Studies in London.

Contact the Author

If you have an angel story, experience or insight and wish to
share it with Theresa, she would love to hear from you. Please
contact her care of Simon and Schuster, 1st Floor, 222 Gray's
Inn Road, London WC1X 8HB or email her at:
angeltalk710@aol.com